The Essential Guide to
Coarse Fishing
in Spain

Philip Pembroke

SANTANA BOOKS

The Essential Guide to Coarse Fishing in Spain
Published by Ediciones Santana, S.L.
Apartado 41
29650 Mijas-Pueblo (Málaga)
Spain

Tel: (0034) 952 48 58 38 Fax: (0034) 952 48 53 67
E-Mail: info@santanabooks.com

Printed in Spain by Gráficas San Pancracio, S.L.

ISBN-13: 978-84-89954-49-6
ISBN-10:   84-89954-49-6

Depósito Legal: MA-1.675/2006

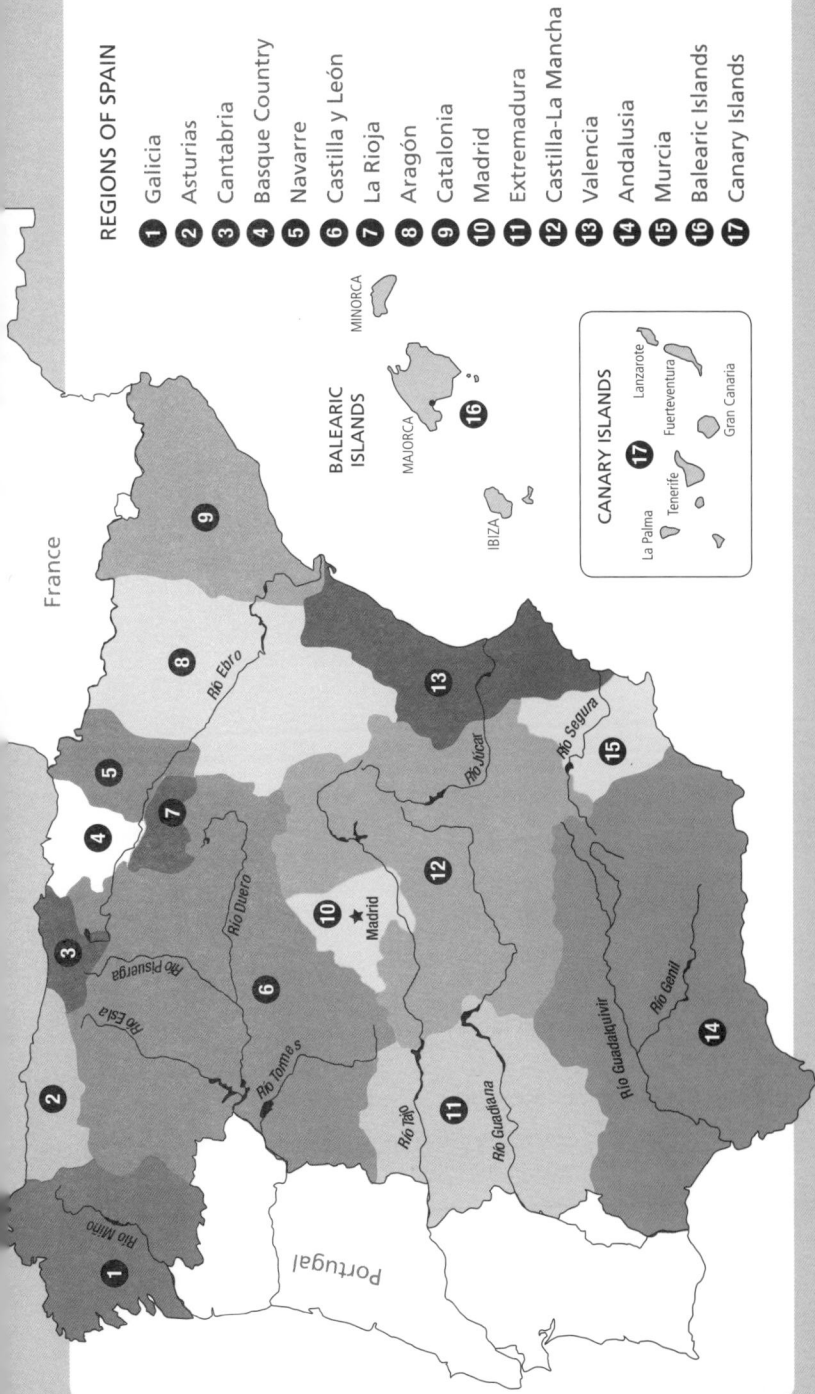

REGIONS OF SPAIN

1. Galicia
2. Asturias
3. Cantabria
4. Basque Country
5. Navarre
6. Castilla y León
7. La Rioja
8. Aragón
9. Catalonia
10. Madrid
11. Extremadura
12. Castilla-La Mancha
13. Valencia
14. Andalusia
15. Murcia
16. Balearic Islands
17. Canary Islands

France

BALEARIC ISLANDS

MINORCA

MAJORCA

IBIZA

CANARY ISLANDS

La Palma

Tenerife

Lanzarote

Fuerteventura

Gran Canaria

Río Ebro

Río Júcar

Río Segura

Río Duero

Río Pisuerga

Río Esla

Río Tormes

Río Miño

Río Tajo

Río Guadiana

Río Guadalquivir

Río Genil

Madrid

Portugal

Contents

⬇ Introduction

Some places mentioned in this guide are way off the beaten track. Access to many more is straightforward and requires less than an hour's drive from the coast. Remember: every location boasts a great angling pedigree. The River Ebro is an example. Offering a unique angling experience, it is the most visited destination in Spain for fishermen and women from northern Europe.

But the rest of the country has plenty to offer. Alicante and Valencia boast the country's premier American largemouth black bass lakes. Andalusia is home to the beautiful gypsy barbel and the Río Guadalquivir hopefully leaves a door open to an infrequent but most welcome visitor, the Atlantic sturgeon.

Because of the diversity of regional dialects and languages most fish will have at least three different names — plus a host of local definitions. It's worth remembering a few. An example: the shad (*sábalo* in Spanish) is called the *zamborca* in Galicia, *kodak* in the Basque Country and *alatja* in Catalonia.

Consulting the A-Z list can terminate endless discussion about some mysterious indigenous fish. Remember its name and later on, in the town bar, expect certain contradiction from the local wag. As an *extranjero* you are not permitted any form of dissent but are encouraged to reward the font with a generous amount of *cerveza* and an appreciative smile.

Fish aren't just found in rivers and lakes in Spain. In the north the fish is a symbol of Christianity. Take a magnificent building like the 12th-century Byzantine cathedral at Zamora: its elegant cupola is covered in fantastic fishtail patterns. Likewise, the Guggenheim museum in Bilbao has a silvery titanium fish-scaled roof.

Around 3,000 British anglers travel to Spain each year. Since they spread themselves over thousands of waterways in an area twice the size of the UK, you are unlikely to bump into many of them. Unless, that is, you attend one of the major international angling championships held in Spain — in which case you will notice quite a few.

Wherever you go, have a good time, but take protection against the sun and heat. Five hours in the burning open during an Andalusian July or August will turn you into a ripe prune. But you won't taste as nice.

Philip Pembroke
October 2006

Fantastic fish-tail patterns on the cathedral at Zamora

Overview

CHAPTER ONE

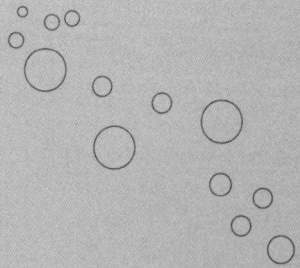

↓ The Iberian Angling Experience

On the surface many species of fish in Spain will seem very familiar, but take a closer look and things start to change.

Many of Iberia's fish are unique. There are not as many fish species as in central Europe but the proportion that are endemic (naturally found nowhere else) is higher. In fact, 45 per cent of the peninsula's fish species are endemic. There is a strong genetic diversity. Iberia's southerly latitude provided many Ice Age refuges that afforded a wide range of niche environments with varied local climates and geography. These played a major role in the isolation of its fish species from the rest of Europe.

Their exclusive evolution gave rise over an extended period to the many distinctive variants of barbel species now found in Spain. Barbel grow bigger here and fight harder than almost anywhere else. The geological age of Iberian river systems is a good indication of how long the fish have been here. Barbel colonised Iberia more than two million years ago from North Africa and eventually gave rise to six endemic species. After the Ice Age the Pyrenean barrier prevented *Barbus barbus*, which had already colonised central Europe from its origins near the Danube delta on the Black Sea, from entering the Iberian Peninsula.

The peninsula's geology has more in common with that of North Africa than Europe. For this reason there are only a handful of natural lakes (*lagos*) in Spain, around 70. France, in comparison, has tens of thousands. The profusion of reservoirs (*embalses*) is a comparatively recent development. But now Spain is the fourth biggest dam-builder in the world. Different water management practices in Iberia affect the distribution of fish species and their behaviour and dictates the tactics anglers need to catch them.

The feeding habits of barbel of the Río Guadiaro in Cádiz Province are affected by the pattern of water extraction by the local orange groves. At 6pm every day irrigation ceases, the current returns and the increased food supply washing down the channel stimulates a feeding spree.

Fish don't fare as well in reservoirs near the Spanish Costas. A sub-tropical climate generates constant spawning conditions that when combined with no natural predation encourages over-population of fish competing for limited food resources. The result is stunted fish growth.

Water levels frequently rise and fall leaving larger fish struggling for oxygen. Aquatic vegetation cannot survive, leading to bare rocky or sandy shores which can look like the surface of the moon. This leaves little protective cover for fish from large hunting birds.

Water quality management is more consistent further inland where high water levels in much bigger reservoirs are carefully controlled to produce hydro- electric power. There is an abundance of natural cover near the shoreline. Fish stand a better chance of survival during periods of drought. Natural predation of smaller fish by stocked black bass and pike promotes a mature population. Fish are fewer in number so the competition for food resources is reduced and they grow larger.

It is a common assumption that Spanish anglers eat everything they catch. Good or bad? Spanish anglers have been bagging their catches throughout history. These traditional water management techniques have proved very effective at maintaining a healthy fish population where natural predation has been absent.

La Pesqueruela is a popular weir swim in the Río Duero. Systematic extraction by local anglers of up to 10 small barbel for the pot over the years has produced a healthy head of large barbel. Not their original intention of course, but of long- term ecological benefit to a stretch of river that might otherwise be suffering from over-population and stunted fish growth. Put simply, regular culling at this location has had the same effect as natural predation in other waters.

On the Iberian peninsula, French-style, eight-hectare (20-acre) managed carp fisheries don't exist. At least, not yet. Carp grow to smaller top-end weights than in France. They are yet to be exposed to artificial baits, which have pushed up unnaturally the north European carp record by 30 per cent in the past 15 years.

> Pound for pound, fish in Spain will fight harder. And, exhibiting a true predatory instinct, their bites are often more aggressive

Fish in Spain grow to their natural maximum weight over a longer period of time. They have not been artificially bulked up in a small stock pond on a crash diet of steroids or proteins. They are therefore more resistant to disease. Pound for pound they will fight harder. And, exhibiting a truer predatory instinct, their bites are often more aggressive.

The Embalse de Orellana (Extremadura) holds the Spanish carp record at around 70lb (32kg). Caught on a Spanish bean. This does not suggest a boilie diet (boilie is a specialist carp angler bait with various flavours, usually made from reconstituted protein or carbohydrate-based artificial foodstuffs). The potential exists for big natural weights comparable to those caught in French waters, but these have not yet been achieved.

↓ Native Fish Species and Guests

One quarter of the fish that you will attempt to catch have been introduced to Spain as guest species. According to the Journal of Fish Biology, 25 fish species have been introduced since 1900, 15 of them since 1945 and eight species since 1990. In many river basins in the region of Catalonia (Catalunya in the Catalan language), the number of invasive species exceeds native ones. In total, Catalan rivers are home to 30 native species and 22 foreign species of fish. The rate of introduction is estimated at one new species per year, and is thought to be increasing.

> Catalan rivers are home to 30 native species and 22 foreign species of fish. The rate of introduction is estimated at one new species per year

The Embalse de Boadella, only 14km from France, has six fish species introduced from France. Bream were stocked in 2004 and will probably spread downstream through the Río Muga river system. Other non-indigenous species found here are perch, roach, zander, and rudd. This reservoir and the Banyoles lake are the main entrance points for exotic freshwater fish into the Iberian peninsula.

Zander (*lucio perca*) were introduced here as a sporting fish in the 1980s, probably from Switzerland, to attract French and German tourists. It spread in rapid fashion to the Ebro, then further south to reservoirs at Buendía, just east of Madrid, and Entrepeñas on the Río Tajo (Madrid). Zander aren't caught any higher up than the tail-end of the Entrepeñas dam. The present population is spectacular. They are caught all year around with a spinner or livebait and average between two and four kilos.

The wild carp is the oldest new arrival. It was introduced to Spain by monasteries for aquaculture in the Middle Ages. Mutant strains bred for the table had shorter, fatter profiles with less scales i.e. commons, mirrors and leathers. Common carp originated in Galicia. Pure wild carp are still evident in some rivers. But don't mistake them for the common carp also found in rivers. They both have a long, lean shape, feral versions having interbred with original wild carp to produce hybrids. The East Asian topmouth gudgeon (*Pseudorasbora parva*) has been recorded for the first time in the Ebro delta via involuntary introduction. Regarded as a pest, it competes with other small fry due to its high reproduction rate. Slow growth rates of native fish due to historic absence of native predators leaves them at a disadvantage.

Stream regulation for irrigation has made dispersal of some visitor species particularly easy in Iberia. The Louisiana (red swamp) crayfish was introduced to southern Spain in 1974 as a good cash crop. In only five years it had spread to the north. As the Spanish prefer eating local seafood, it is now regarded as a dangerous pest. It displaces the native species of crayfish, which can only survive in cold mountain streams, it undermines riverbanks and it devours the stems of young rice plants, a major Spanish crop.

Pike were introduced in 1949 with mixed results. They can be found in the Duero, Tajo, Guadiana, Júcar, Segura, Llobregat and Ebro, and in many reservoirs less than 1,000 metres above sea-level. A study of those in the Lagunas de Ruidera in Castilla-La Mancha has found that their size is directly related to the amount of red swamp crayfish ingested. Unfortunately, all native prey species have disappeared due to pike predation in these lakes except the endangered Iberian blenny (*Blennius fluviatilis*).

A recent arrival is the pumpkinseed or sun fish (*Lepomis gibbosus*), known as pez sol or perca sol in Spain. It looks like a perch but has a mottled shiny colour. Its introduction from North America in the 1970s coincided with a spurt in dam construction and the tenacious little predator has colonised at a phenomenal rate. The world record is 0.63kg from Mexico. The average in Iberia is 0.05kg and 20cm in length. It feeds on invertebrates and small fish. It is here to stay and can now be found all over Spain. Lago Banyoles has the fastest growing pumpkinseed population on the Iberian peninsula. It has had a catastrophic effect on native fauna as it eats indigenous fish eggs and competes for food.

The spread of black bass is not a particular problem since in general they are restricted to main reservoirs where they can find prey fish.

Angling tourism has been responsible for the introduction of many species. In 1974 Roland Lorkowsky, a German biologist and fishing nut, released a few thousand fry of wels catfish (*Silurus glanis*) into the Río Ebro at Flix. Adapting very well to these warm murky waters, the catfish has now extended its range up to the Río Segre (Lleida) and the Río Cinca (Huesca). It has also colonised Lago Banyoles and Lago de Sau (Girona). By common consent its voracious eating habits have been catastrophic for many native species. It has been officially stocked by Portugal's Serviços Florestais in the Alentejo's huge new Barragem Alqueva.

The mosquitofish (*Gambusia*) is one of the few examples of a positive introduction. Released in 1921 to combat malaria, it played no small part in the eradication of the disease over the next 40 years. Incidentally, it is probably the most widespread freshwater fish in the world.

Native species have evolved over millennia into niche environments, and are sensitive to sudden changes in environment brought about by aggressive newcomers. Some of these new fish species are extremely well-suited to conditions in Catalan rivers, especially in zones rich in nutrients and are progressively pushing out local species.

The strong genetic diversity of native Spanish brown trout is under threat from restocking with too similar strains. Overall numbers are declining in the wild due to over-fishing. The native trout is being crowded out of Spanish rivers by the aggressive rainbow trout, although it is not yet endangered. Attempts to restock rivers with non-indigenous brown trout (132 trout farms nationally) have reduced the diversity of the native gene pool, resulting in reduced fertility and resistance to disease.

One exception is in Galicia. Here restocking is carried out with greater subtlety, e.g. breeding hybrid strains by introducing genetically distinct German brown trout. Cessation of stocking elsewhere has had a positive effect on the native gene pool. The answer: keep daily angling quotas but increase size limits, to increase the mature native breeding gene pool.

Research into effects of exotic fish introductions on native species is gaining currency. At the Vega del Guadiana nursery near Badajoz all fish species native to Extremadura are being bred, including barbel, *bogas* (nase) and *pardillas* (mini-carp).

The "introduce anything" sentiment is now out of style. Even so, piranhas are reported on the loose. Spain's current neglect of its biological resources as represented by the brown trout is breaking international agreements it has signed. But it is not the only country at fault.

↓ Ecological Issues

Water use: Spain is fourth in the world dam-building league. The Ebro is the most dammed river in Spain. It supplies 50 per cent of Spain's energy through hydro-electric plants.

The question of water diversion from the wet North to the dry South (the dryness is a myth perpetuated by the government) is a big political issue. In 1993, the Spanish government announced a national water plan, the Plan Hidrológico Nacional. To cost around 18 billion euros in today's currency, it was Spain's great opportunity, they said, without specifying for what. The plan, which first appeared 60 years ago, was scrapped in 2004 by the new Socialist government, and the proposed "*trasvase del Ebro*", the channelling of Ebro water south, abandoned. Instead, plans were announced to construct a series of huge desalinisation plants along the Mediterranean coast.

> The Ebro's flow at its mouth is 22% less than in 1971. This is probably true of many other big rivers around Europe. But that doesn't make it right. So much for ecology...

Presently, 85 per cent of water diverted is used for agriculture, but 50 per cent of this is lost through bad management and old-fashioned irrigation ideas. Valencia, a potential beneficiary, has plenty of its own underground water, but it's been polluted by industry. Valencia, however, continues to insist the "*trasvase*" is essential and maintains that every year the Ebro empties into the sea 30 times as much water as what they are asking for.

The government sees water as a commodity not a resource. Water flowing into the sea is money wasted. Dams upstream are causing the Ebro delta to sink. In 1940 20 million tonnes of silt were deposited at the delta, but in 1978 only three million tonnes, the rest being deposited in calm water above the hydro- electric dams. The Ebro's flow at its mouth is 22 per cent less than in 1971.This is probably true of many other big rivers around Europe. But that doesn't make it right. So much for ecology. For more information, go to www.rivernet.org.

Pollution: In the spring of 2001 five sites along the lower Río Ebro (Spain's biggest river) showed presence of endocrine-disrupting chemicals in sewage discharges and industrial contaminants, measuring up to 1,400 ng/g (levels of DDT pesticides — nanogrammes per gramme). Water with 50-400ng/g is regarded as highly contaminated.

A chemical spill in 2001 from an electrochemical plant on the Río Ebro at Flix caused high mercury pollution which resulted in thousands of fish deaths. However, while the delayed maturation of female carp and the sterilisation of male carp may also be caused by the presence of alkyl phenol waste from the Flix factory, this is unlikely to be the sole cause. The depressed levels of testosterone in carp samples is blamed equally on the outflows below Zaragoza's sewage treatment plant.

In April 1998 the rupture of a tailings pond at Aznalcollar mine (35km west of Seville) resulted in 4,634 hectares of rivers and land being covered in up to 15cm of toxic waste for a distance of 40km. Aquatic life was depleted and vegetation devastated. Nevertheless, carp and otter returned within two years to the Frailes, Agrio and Guadiamar rivers due to a prompt and effective cleanup and there are apparently no long-term effects.

↓ Practicalities

FISHING LICENCE AND ANGLING REGULATIONS

Do I need a licence to fish in Spain?
Yes, it is a mandatory purchase. In general it can be obtained from any local office of the Delegación de la Agencia Medio Ambiente (AMA). You will need your passport or driving licence. The provincial coarse angling licence costs around €12.50 and only covers an individual Spanish province for one year, minimum, but is valid for two rods. If you are over 65, you will get it free for up to four years. Under-16s go free. Details on where to purchase one are given for each area discussed in the guide. Some areas require, in addition, the purchase of an insurance

coupon; ask when you purchase your licence. Andalusia requires an exam or proof of experience (see section on Andalusia). You can order your Spanish provincial angling licence on-line. However, offices go on holiday in August. Cost is €15, plus €2 post inside Spain. By arrangement from U.K. Visit:
www.sulicencia.com/licenciapesca.htm#solicitarpesca

Is it costly to fish in Spain?
Most waters are free. Where not, the cost of a day ticket is usually very reasonable. The coarse fishing season in Spain is year-around.

Can I fish from a boat?
To use a boat on freshwater reservoirs and rivers, a boat licence is usually required. Apply to the water board (*confederación hidrográfica*) in the province you wish to fish. This insures the user of the vessel and fellow-passengers for the area the water authority covers.

Where restrictions may apply
There are two types of free zones, or *zonas libres*, and they are well signposted:
Zonas libres en régimen tradicional (free zones with traditional rules) – normal bag limit and use of all permitted baits.
Zonas libres sin muerte (free zones without death)
 – artificial baits only, fish must be returned alive and in good condition.

Zonas de Régimen Especial are zones controlled by special regulations of local water authorities. They are divided into areas signposted as:
Vedados de Pesca, private fishing reserves in which, temporarily or permanently, all fishing is prohibited or fishing of a particular species is banned; or *Cotos de Pesca* (literally "fishing reserves"), where leisure angling is regulated in the interests of sustainable management. Permission needs to be obtained to fish these cotos.
Zonas de protección especial are zones containing valuable fish types, special landscape or fauna that require special protection.
Refugios de pesca are refuges that serve as spawning grounds, where angling is forbidden.
Reservas genéticas are reserves where the gene pool of indigenous fish species and their biodiversity are protected. Fishing may be banned (*vedado*) here or a reserve may be classed as *zona libre sin muerte* or *coto sin muerte* (see explanation below).

Fishing reserves, or *Cotos de pesca*, are classed as follows:
Cotos de pesca intensivos (intensive fishing reserves), bag limit

permitted, periodic stocking required; *Cotos de pesca sin muerte* (reserve of fishing without death), all fish must be returned alive in good condition; *Cotos de pesca en régimen tradicional* (fishing reserves with traditional regulations), bag limit permitted. A *Coto privado* is privately owned water. Here day tickets may be purchased, usually from a nearby town bar.

A water described as a "fishing reserve with special regulations" is a mix of coarse and game fishing. The water co-exists as a game fishing area. A game angling licence is required for trout, which may only be caught here on artificial lures. On these hybrid waters the angling season for trout is from March 19 to August 31 lowlands (*bajo montaña*) and from May 14 to September 30 highlands (*alto montaña*). Coarse angling is permitted year around. The fishing reserves are day ticket.

Warning: A sign stating that water depth varies doesn't indicate that the lake bed is uneven. It means that the water level will vary because of dam activity. Park a safe distance away from the bank as this means the water level can change dramatically over just a few hours. Contact the local river authority for latest information on the water that you wish to visit.

See each region for the addresses of the relevant authorities.

How do I find the best swims?
This book gives directions to help you find some of Spain's finest fishing spots. Useful sketch maps detailing the location of the swims in each region are available on the author's website: **www.spainfishing.com**

The website offers other useful information, including details of expatriate angling clubs. Readers with any queries about angling in Spain can email the author at philippembroke007@hotmail.com

Aragón

Catalonia

Gerona

Lérida

Río Ebro

Zaragoza

Fayón

Barcelona

Calatayud

EMBALSE DE
MEQUINEZA

Flix

Tarragona

Teruel

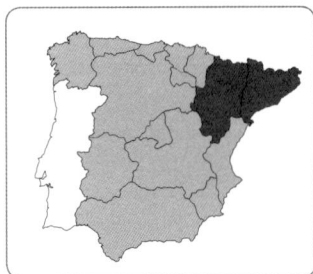

Catalonia-Aragón

CHAPTER TWO

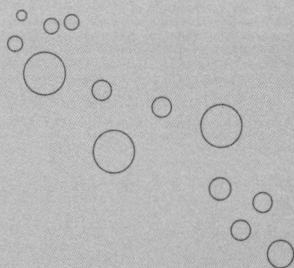

⬇ River Ebro

The Ebro gets pride of place because it has some of the best sport fishing on the Iberian peninsula. This is the real Spain and good fishing here coincides with tasty food and drink, a rewarding local culture and some great scenery. The Ebro is Spain's premier waterway. It rises in the Cantábrica mountain range, south of Santander, and flows 928 kilometres across northern Spain to its delta in the Mediterranean, about 160 kilometres south of Barcelona.

I first fished the Ebro in 1989 and have returned on many occasions since. It covers a big area, too big to fish all the waters in one trip. There are hundreds of places to visit and this fantastic area is easy to navigate. The Ebro stays in view from the road along most of the suggested route, as you rarely leave this beautiful valley.

Angling here can offer better value for money than spending an expensive weekend on syndicated water in the UK. There are three levels of expenditure to consider:

1. Day trips with catfish charter boats. The most expensive option, but well worth it if you have never caught a fish weighing in excess of 40lb. A lot of those "celebrities" pictured in the national press holding huge catfish will have gone down this route. As well as the boat and tackle, you are paying for local expertise. After all, these catfish guys do this for a living. See below for details.

2. All-inclusive angling holidays. They cost more but it works out cheaper on a daily basis. Typically, you pay for accommodation near the water, provision of licences and tackle if requested, baits and transport. Some will have full-time hosts and offer a range of other activities. Newcomers to the region may appreciate their on-the-spot angling advice. All these companies are on the Internet.

3. Do it yourself. This can be the cheapest option, the one preferred by the author. The advantage is greater flexibility. You have the freedom to choose where to stay each night. You get to fish over a wider area. By the way, the big catfish are just as easy to hook into from the bank. It's landing them that's always the problem.

As you travel upstream, the scenery changes. From the coast up to

Xerta there is a fertile plain. The contrast between the lime-rich soil of the surrounding hills and the intense greenness of the valley, with large-scale market gardening, is quite extraordinary. The river system is divided into three regions. From the delta to the weir at Tiverneys, it is known as the Baix d'Ebre. Upstream is known as the Móra d'Ebre. From Móra to Flix you have the Ribera d'Ebre.

Where the Ebro cuts through the Catalan hills upstream, you will encounter spectacular steep gorges. Boats cannot navigate above Miravet. Beyond Móra the barren landscape takes on a grand scale. Enjoy yourself but respect the river. The surrounding environment, nature and wildlife, is a complete contrast to what you find when fishing your local water. All along the banks are copses of white poplar, alder, ash and water willow, as well as eucalyptus and locust trees. At dusk, you'll witness kingfishers, herons, buzzards, egrets, eagles and brown terns.

If you have common sense, you will do well. The fish here are the same as everywhere else, if a touch less sophisticated. That does not mean easier. Your skills will count.

Because the conditions on the river change seasonally, and annually, no honest guide will guarantee big catches. As long as you do not expect large bags as of right, a nice specimen will come as a bonus to the wonderful experience that is the Ebro.

Reaching the Ebro

Access is easy. Scheduled and charter flights to Barcelona and Reus airports are available from most UK regional airports. The river is two hours south by car or train. From Barcelona airport you head south on the A7 motorway and exit at Junction 40 for Tortosa and 41 for Amposta and St Carles de la Ràpita. Within 10 minutes of exiting the motorway, you can be at the river bank.

By train, go from Barcelona airport to Sants railway station in the city, where you change for Tortosa. It is a relaxing journey along the Costa Dorada coastline. At Tortosa, walk the 400 metres to the Ebro or hail a taxi to scenic Xerta from near the railway station. Reus airport is even nearer to the Ebro and a taxi ride to Tarragona rail station will connect you quickly to Tortosa. →

➜ If you're holidaying on the coast, access is easy from, for example, Salou. Just hop on the motorway and drive one hour south to Tortosa (exit the A7 at junction 40). Start your fishing right away, in town or at Xerta.

The Ebro delta (Delta de l'Ebre) is a good place to base yourself since the river fishes well all the way down to the sea. You can walk along empty beaches, visit one of the commercial (dorada) fish farms at feeding time, try one of the famous local seafood specialities.

The delta is a big rice-growing area but also a nature park with the most important aquatic wildlife environment in the western Mediterranean, rivalling the Camargue in France. Sixty per cent of bird species found in Europe can be seen at the delta and nine out of 10 waterfowl that winter in the Catalonia region (Catalunya) do so there. Flamingos are a highlight, as are spoonbills, purple gallinules and cattle egrets. Spot them from the many bird hides provided for tourists. Delta information: www.ebre.com/delta has good pictures and words on the environment.

Another form of wild life includes smuggling, a feature of the Ebro delta for hundreds of years. From time to time the Guardia Civil intercepts boats as they attempt to land at delta ports their "catches" of cannabis resin and similar substances weighing thousands of kilos.

For those of us seeking big fish of another kind, Tortosa, just north of the delta, is a handy base. The local bus service is cheap and very reliable and will connect you to all the spots mentioned in the Ebro area.

If you want to be near the sea, Sant Carles de la Ràpita is a great place to stay. It combines all the amenities of a quality family beach resort, with easy access to all of your favourite angling locations. Its restaurants specialise in tasty seafood dishes. And there is no Macdonalds in sight. Tackle shop at St Carles: L'Anarin, Pesca Esportiva, Jesus, 13. Tel. 977 740946. Tourist Office: Pl. Carles lll, 13, 43540 Sant Carles de la Ràpita. Tel. 977 740 100, 977 744 624. Fax 977 744 387. Email: turisme@larapita.com Information at www.larapita.com, www.ebre.com/larapita

For the best camping location, with a nice restaurant (order mussels for lunch) and good facilities, try Mediterani Blau Camping at Platja dels

Eucaliptus, Amposta. Tel. 977 478 095 & 977 479 046. Fifteen minutes from St Carles and on the beach at the delta. Travelling back, use the ferry at Sant Jaume d'Enveja to cross the Ebro. There's a good campsite with apartments at Alcanar Platja just south of St Carles. Tel. 977 740 561. Email: info@alfaques.com, www.alfaques.com

↓ Ebro Fish Species

Carp

Common carp are the dominant species. They average 2-3kg, but many grow much bigger. Beautiful specimens over 10kg are a familiar sight. They are much sleeker than their fatter, lake-bound cousins. Mirror carp are also caught here to even bigger sizes. Ebro carp as you will find out are fighting fit and fight hard. Use Raptor hooks (barbless). Do not bother with the Spanish Mustad hooks. The smaller carp are kamikaze pilots, put up a good fight and easily straighten out Mustads.

I suggest 20lb minimum braided line for serious carp fishing. Braid shears through the weed well. The big carp, 30lb-plus old timers, put their heads down and go — right out into the deep middle channel. Accept that they will empty your spool on the first run (50 metres) as there is nothing you can do about it. Baits to use are sweetcorn and luncheon meat. Trout/salmon pellets or pastes often work better than boilies. For carp, use heavy feeder rods 1.5-2.5lb test curve.

Catfish whoppers

The River Ebro is renowned throughout Europe for the quality of its catfish angling. You may have seen a photo of a big catfish in your local tackle shop. It was almost certainly caught on the Ebro.

The Spanish record is 197lb, caught on the Upper Ebro at Mequinenza in September 2002 by Glen Patterson from Tamworth. He took 35 minutes to land the two-metres specimen. This fish was safely

returned, but it could have fed 300 people. Many more are caught in excess of 100lb. The British record is just 65lb.

The record for the Lower Ebro stands at 165lb, landed at the end of 2002 by Emille Hjeteberg from Sweden. At present Emille is studying for a doctorate in marine biology, so there can be no argument that he is considerably cleverer than the fish he caught that day. The average caught weight on the Lower Ebro is between 80lb and 120lb. This high score is due to the abundance of the local food supply, mullet. On the Upper Ebro, e.g. at Mequinenza, where the food supply is relatively scarce, the average is much lower.

Two species of catfish are found here, the wels (*Silurus glanis*) and the Channel cat.

The world record for a wels — the biggest of the world's 2,000 species of catfish — is 306 kilos. Their prey includes fish, frogs, ducks and voles. They are cannibalistic. And some will even try to bite humans. On large Russian lakes the locals use baby pigs as bait. During 2001 in Germany, one of these monsters reportedly ate a dachshund puppy as it played

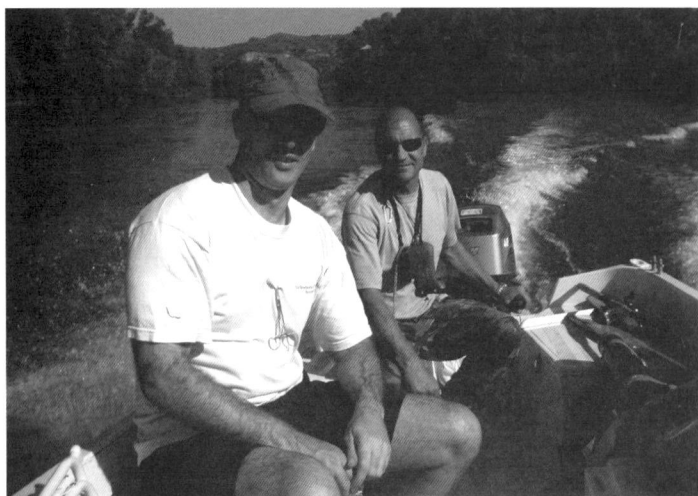

PHOTO COURTESY OF PAUL DELANHEY

The author catfishing on the Ebro at Miravet, with John Campion of www.ebroboathire.com

lakeside at the Volksgarten Park in Muenchen Gladbach. Why wasn't it on a lead? Sadly, this 1.8-metre piscatorial terrorist, known locally as Kuno the Killer, was found dead on July 25, 2003. However its fame lives on in the name of a local rock band, Kuno's Friends. Just for the record, it's illegal to lasso a catfish in the states of Tennessee and Washington.

Catfish aren't pretty, but beauty is in the eye of the beholder. Numbers vary from year to year and during a season. 2002 was a vintage year. February is very good, as is April, and they will come good again in September. A boat or dinghy is often used to fish catfish. Fishing from the bank is a good alternative. Do not be tempted to use lighter gear — once hooked, they can take hours to land. Take the largest landing net you can handle. Bite alarms come in handy, but are not essential.

> Catfish aren't pretty but beauty is in the eye of the beholder – once hooked they can take hours to land

Use 80lb braided line. Livebait only, on bottle rigs, from the bank. Fish deadbaits with floats. From the boat it's ok to fish both methods. To make a bottle rig, fix a Coke bottle (half-filled with water) to the line about three feet from a very big hook. Attach an 80lb wire leader with a weight heavy enough to set the bottle. Chuck everything into the channel as far as you can. If the rod is unsupervised, fix it to something substantial so the catfish can't pull it in. Set the clutch loosely, á la bait-runner-style. Then tighten it up after the strike. But remember, these fish are more than capable of pulling you in, so watch your step!

Sea bass
Yes, they are a saltwater species, but will run all the way up to the weir at Tiverneys. They average 4lb, can grow to 20lb, a 12lb specimen is not uncommon. July might be early for them. Usually they run late June to mid- August. These are the silver fish you will have seen at dusk going after the surface fry. Bass go after your "Black Sophies" lures.

Zander
These will feed very close in — 15lb is a good fish. They will strip your line off, but, once the run is over, pull them out. They will not take a resistant line. Leave it slack and deadbait downstream. The bite will tighten the line. But then the fish will certainly run towards you. So watch out. Try a spinner. You never know.

American largemouth black bass

Some good individual specimens to 5lb surrounded by a lot of smaller chaps. Lures to use include minnow patterns and rubber shads. If weed is a problem, go for surface lures. Try a big S. The national record stands at 4kg (8.8lb), caught at the Embalse de Gaudalcacín, near Cádiz in 2001.

Mullet

Caught up to 15lb. The record is 30lb. They are found around the sewage outflow pipes of towns and villages. Catch them with breaded float on light tackle, for a good fight.

Other species

Pumpkinseed (*perca sol*), a type of sunfish, is an introduced species and just like the piranha, a flesh-eater. Try small deadbait. You will find bream in the slower water along with chub. **Tuna**, although uncommon, are caught here. **Crucian** to 5lb, **roach** and **rudd** to 5lb at Miravet. **Barbel** are the hardest fighting fish in the river. They disappeared completely from the Lower Ebro in a five-year period during the early 1990s. This is not consistent with the catfish predation argument because catfish distribution has remained uneven. Though they have had a sizable effect on the pattern of fish stocks in general, it's highly unlikely that catfish prefer the taste of barbel in preference to all other species.

Barbel's disappearance could have been caused by construction, such as installation of boat locks at Tiverneys which have undermined sensitive spawning conditions by altering the flow rate. Barbel have re-colonised the Lower Ebro from the healthy feeder streams. Or have catfish tastes moved on?

Tackle and tactics

You will not need fancy rigs. If truth were told, you can fish with the most rudimentary tactics and be successful. The fish here are usually untouched and comparatively unsophisticated. They will not normally have been caught before.

A simple running paternoster rig for carp and barbel will get you excellent results. As mentioned, hair and bolt rigs are often used to present commercial carp baits. Feeder methods can more accurately deliver groundbait in the faster channels, and at distance. Pole fishing is worth a go e.g. at Flix. I have witnessed a 7kg common carp landed with one here. But make sure your leader is up to the job.

Rules

- No night fishing

- No camping by bankside

- No fires

- The Guardia Civil may confiscate your fishing gear if you fail to comply and return it only on payment of a fine.

- A fishing licence is mandatory, as is fishing insurance.

- Two-rod limit.

These regulations are most strictly enforced at Riba-roja and Mequinenza, where there is a water bailiff. Elsewhere there is normally a more relaxed approach to the rules. If in doubt, ask locally.

For all enquiries about the Ebro, e.g. water levels, pollution, boat licences, illegal dynamiting etc, contact:

Confederación Hydrográfica del Ebro
Paseo de Segasta, 24-26, 50071 Zaragoza

Tel: 976 221 993. Email: webmaster@chebro.es. www.chebro.es

⬇ Favourite Swims on the Lower Ebro

Here are some of my favourite spots. They are graded to suit anglers with varying ability and mobility. Note: Journey times are given for a start at Tortosa.

Grade A: the swim is suitable for anglers of all abilities and ages with easy access to the bank.

Grade B: older and younger sports may find access a problem.

Grade C: some may find the fishing to be harder than at other places, access may require a greater than average level of stamina.

Peter Sales, who has lived, worked, and fished the Ebro for many years, recommends Tortosa as a good place to start your adventure. "There are easily found good swims, on both banks containing, nice carp and all the other species mentioned."

Peter recalls: "The first catfish I saw was by looking over the river wall at Tortosa. It must have gone to 50lb. The size of the big carp is gob-smacking. Look over the wall at the tackle shop in town (by the old bridge). Here the outflow pipe attracts hundreds of mullet, and you have a good chance of spotting a catfish as it comes up for dinner. Enormous sea bass here also take the small mullet."

If you are a catfish virgin, we urge you to contact Peter Sales for expert advice. You can email your questions straight to his permanent home, right on the Ebro (fishytales@hotmail.com). He will be more than happy to pass on his unrivalled knowledge of angling in Spain direct to you, free of charge. Danny Sales (Peter's son) organises angling holidays from Bitem on the Ebro. His website: www.catfishingriverebro.com

---

Licences

Purchase your angling licence from: Generalitat de Catalunya, Edificio Sabate (2nd floor), Carrer Ramon Berenguer IV, Tortosa. Near the underground car park next door to banks.
Further information: Tourist Office, Pl. del Bimil-lenari, s/n, Tortosa. Tel/fax. 977 510 822.

To purchase or hire tackle, visit Germans Arbo, Caça i Pesca, Sant Isidre,176, Tortosa (by the old bridge). Tel. 977 740 260.

Swims around Tortosa

Tortosa offers several good swims, all with safe parking close to the river. The right bank opposite the Civil War monument is gravel and fishable for well over 200 metres. This is a popular local match venue and should be avoided at weekends. On the left bank, starting some 200 metres above the monument is a grassed meadow that offers good fishing for over 50 pegs. Also on the left bank, but about half a kilometre downstream is a landing platform. Just below this platform is a gravel bank, then a meadow that offers several hundred metres of comfortable fishing.

Chickenhole Swim (C: 10 minutes): The swim is named after the effluent pipe coming from the nearby chicken factory. If you can smell something awful, you are there. Mullet feed on the chicken waste; catfish feed on the mullet. Carp here (they just come for the company)

PHOTO COURTESY OF ROB AND MARGARET WWW.EBROTOURS.COM

River Ebro at Tortosa looking southwest

average 6lb (2.8 kilos). If you find yourself overwhelmed by the stink, remember to direct your discharge in the direction of the channel — it will attract the specimens you seek. Directions: from Tortosa take the C12 (TV3443) road to Amposta, about seven minutes or three kilometres, past a row of plane trees and a bar-restaurant on the right, to a chicken factory on right. Turn left straight away, 500 metres down to the river. If coming the other way, turn left off the main road, then cross over right to the dirt track. Park in the space provided and walk 20 metres down to the bank.

Norman's Island Swim (odour-free) (A: 10 minutes): Named after a popular local English angler, now deceased, whose spirit it is said will protect you from vengeful chickens. Please note: Norman's Island is not an island. At centre is a shallow shingle ramp. Fish in the pools either side. Fish downstream, tight to the bank for good carp. Directions: as for the Chickenhole. Park as for the Chickenhole but go left down to bank.

Canal de l'Esquerra de l'Ebre (on right bank) (A): Take my word for it: you will be amazed by the quantity of fish here. Fish with a 2oz lead to hold tight against flow. Barbel are found where the flow exits a tunnel or under a bridge. Fish downstream of these features, where a deeper hole exists before sediment sinks to the channel bottom.

Directions: choose any spot from Tiverneys down to Amposta. Just pull off the T301 and head a few hundred metres through the olive groves, in the direction of the Ebro.

PHOTO COURTESY OF DANNY SALES

This large carp, held by Danny Sales, is in excess of 13kg

Bitem Landing (B: 15 minutes): Fishing here can be hard, but on a good day very rewarding as all species in the river can be caught, carp, mullet, roach, black bass. A good all-round swim. Due to the shallow water and fast current, this is a good spot for sea bass when running. Dawn and dusk are best. A lazy way to fish is to put a float by the jetty (a metre deep). Due to the back eddy, carp will come right up under your feet. Some are massive, up to 40 lb. Further out, look at the water for a crease line, the border between fast water and slack. Here at about 30 metres out, the riverbed slopes off. Cast on to it. Directions: 4km from Tortosa, on the T301 (C42) to Tiverneys. Turn left at the Coop. Go 500 metres down to the river through the smallholdings. Bitem has a good boat ramp, and was dredged comparatively recently. Warning: the mosquitoes at dusk are bad boys here. As this coincides with the best time for fishing, cover yourself in repellent and wear long sleeves/trousers and a hat. Visit: www.tortosa.altanet.org, then click on "bitem".

K3 – 1st swim (C:10 minutes): This spot, just north of Tortosa on the east bank, is brilliant for zander. A 20lb 6oz specimen was caught here recently. This is a black bass swim. Fishing is good all day. Use feeder methods, groundbait heavily (this is a big river). You can buy sweetcorn and luncheon meat locally or use commercial carp baits. Cattle feed used as groundbait can be bought locally as well.

High-tech, weed-cutting boat at Amposta

Directions: take the T301 (C42) from Tortosa towards Bitem. At the 3km marker, turn right and come round and down under the new bridge.

K3 (2nd swim): Big catfish, big carp, 30lb-plus commons and royals (French). Good roach and rudd. There has been a bad weed problem due to low water levels. High water will wash this through every three months. Otherwise use a rake. Hooked carp will head straight for the reedbeds. Fishing is better September onwards when there is less weed.

Ebro feeder streams: These rise in the adjacent hills. They produce decent carp, barbel, and trout. In the summer, mountain streams become dry riverbeds. In small plunge pools, you can spot tiny trout by your feet. Further up the valleys, deeper pools hold big barbel and trout. Buy a good local map. Wear walking boots. If wearing shorts, I advise the use of gaiters. The undergrowth may prove prickly. When wearing waders, use felt bottoms to avoid slipping. Advice: take lots of water and sun protection. Details of two locations follow.

Riu Sénia (C:30 minutes): *Pesca sin muerte* (rainbow trout, barbel, carp). Clear and fast water. Good access. Fish at the water gauge station by the bridge at Masil Molina Abad, just north of Sénia. Fly fishing only allowed from March 15 to August 31. A lot of thick bankside vegetation. Fish in the Pantà d'Ulldecona, north of Molina, for royal carp of every size, year around. Directions: exit A7 at Tortosa, take the TV3421 to La Sénia. The river is north, out of town in direction of Pantà d'Ulldecona.

La Sénia is at the foot of the Els Ports range, a nature park with mountain goats, wildcats, boar, vultures, and freshwater swimming. For expert advice, contact Rob and Margaret (guided walking tours, watercolour painting of flora and fauna). They offer bed and breakfast in their lovely finca near Tortosa. www.ebrotours.co.uk. Email: enquires@ebrotours.co.uk

Swims at Amposta

The next three swims are all accessible from Amposta. By car from Tortosa, take the main road south (C12) to Amposta and the Ebro delta. It takes 25 minutes and Amposta is signposted. By bus use the morning service (same journey time) from the bus station, across from the Tortosa rail station.

Amposta, an agricultural town (population 60,000) in the centre of the delta, backs on to the river. You look across a 300-metre-wide channel. There is a 24- hour packing factory on the opposite bank to the town and, as you stand at Swim 2, the noisy A7 bridge crosses the Ebro to your right. To your left is the Amposta suspension bridge. The people are friendly and hospitable and the high street, Avda. de la Rápita, is good for shops, restaurants and bars. There is a tackle shop halfway along the south side.

You can purchase your angling licence by the Amposta boat slip: Generalitat de Catalunya office, Agriculture and Fisheries Dept, Saint Joan, 41, 43870 Amposta. Tel. 977 701 895. Tourist Office (by the boat slip), Avda. St Jaume, 1, 43870 Amposta. Tel. 977 703 453. Email: info@turismeamposta.org. www.turisme.amposta.altanet.org

Amposta is a centre for boat trips, sea fishing, hiking, caving, mountain biking, canyoning, climbing, diving and sailing. The large rowing club by Swim 2 is popular with British rowing teams as a first-class, warm-weather, winter training destination. Don't ask after the Oxford light rowing crew. In 1998 the 12-man crew was arrested by the Amposta police and deported from Spain for allegedly trying to evade the team's gigantic Pizza Hut bar bill, which totalled 800 euros. A mighty feast, making you wonder how each crew member managed to weigh in at less than 154 pounds as required by international rowing regulations. The municipal authorities alleged 23 separate instances of wilful disobedience, but – in a gesture of sporting goodwill – the crew was invited back the following year.

> The lower Ebro experiences a wind called the Mistral... conditions change from tranquil to deadly (70mph) in less than a minute. Take it seriously; anglers should retreat immediately.

The Lower Ebro experiences a wind called the Mistral, the little brother of the famous Catalan *tramuntana*. It blows from the northwest every couple of months in the summer and has gusted through the lives of many fishermen. Conditions change from tranquil to deadly (70mph) in less than a minute. Take it seriously; anglers should retreat immediately.

Swim 1 (A: 20 minutes): Arriving by car, you find the suspension bridge is half a kilometre on the left as you enter Amposta. You can park in the town centre or off-road over the bridge. On foot, the bus stop is 200 metres from the bridge. After crossing the bridge, immediately head down right into a field. Please take the annual growth of vegetation into account. Walk downstream, parallel to the river, into a farmyard and then down to the pontoon. This swim is about 200 metres downstream from the bridge as the crow flies.

Fishing is good all day. Use feeder methods, groundbait heavily (this is a big river). You can buy sweetcorn and luncheon meat locally. For groundbait, buy a sack of cattle feed from a local farm shop or cooperative. You can then add your own flavour concentrates. Last night's paella is a good option. All these baits are good for the other swims.

Swim 2 (A: 20 minutes): Amposta has a new one-way system for the town, making life more complicated. Follow the signs from the town bridge and circumnavigate Amposta to the south, then east, and back up north, to the riverbank. The map will give you an idea for orientation. The pontoon is in front of you and a concrete bank to the right. Behind is the rowing club and fire station. By bus, get off at the stop 200 metres from the bridge mentioned above, and walk down to the riverbank, to the right of the bridge, on Major Saint Joan. Walk 400 metres downstream along the riverside to the pontoon at the rowing club. Much easier!

Fishing here in the afternoon can be slow. Big carp come up close to the concrete bank in late afternoon. I advise setting groundbait or loosebait two hours before fishing. Boilies work superbly here. The smellier the better. Try salmon and trout pellet/pastes.

Swim 3 (C: 20 minutes): This is the canal outflow drain. Known to locals as The Gusher. On approaching the town, from Tortosa, turn left opposite the petrol station. Go over the canal and 400 metres along to the pumping station. You have to climb down to the drain. I found using a free line with one swan shot baited with breadflake produced good results. You will be able to see the fish as they fall down the sluice, from the canal into the inlet.

Sant Jaume d'Enveja (A: 40 minutes): Fish by the ferry area. Take your kids to this spot because there is always plenty going on. Directions: from Amposta take either TV 3454a or TV 3403 east to the delta. Fish by the ferry on either bank. An outflow pipe attracts mullet and catfish. Catch mullet on light float tackle for a good fight, or try "snigging". Use a large treble hook on 8lb line with a bit of lead weight fixed to the shank. Let it fall for two seconds then whip the rod back and snig the fish anywhere on the body. The Spanish pull mullet out in great numbers.

> This is the spot to witness the Ebro's large catfish. Every so often you will see a huge mouth appear from the depths, amongst the swarming hordes...having partaken of breakfast/elevenses/dinner, the catfish exits with a swish of its powerful tail...

This is the spot to witness the Ebro's large catfish. Every so often you will see a huge open mouth appear from the depths, amongst the swarming horde. There is a big commotion as hundreds of prey fish scatter. Having partaken of breakfast/elevenses/dinner, the catfish exits with a swish of its powerful tail and heads down to the bottom. These mullet must be the most stupid fish around, since a minute later they all return to the pipe as if nothing ever happened. At times this ritual repeats every 15 minutes. It is well worth investigating.

⬇ Catfish Records

Gary Sheridan and his wife Loring run a successful angling holiday business, from their base at Deltebre, on the north bank of the river opposite Sant Jaume d'Enveja. Gary notes: "As a guide it's my job to take anglers to the best fishing hotspots in the area. Access here to the Lower Ebro can prove problematic, as much of the bankside is privately owned. Paradoxically, the fishing is excellent, with several catfish possible in one night over the 100lb mark."

Hard to fish areas are Gary's specialty. "Around Amposta, a few kilometres upstream from our base, specialist tactics are required to fish an area infamous for its snaggy bottom. Livebait tied off to a buoy rig over the top of an obstacle-strewn catfish hole is a deadly method. But be prepared to lose a few. Speed is of the essence here since rigs and hooks often need to be quickly adjusted to match the ever-changing conditions that are a key feature of the Lower Ebro."

Gary's boat once landed seven cats in a single nocturnal session. All fell to eels on single hooks, using casting rigs that pop the bait up off the →

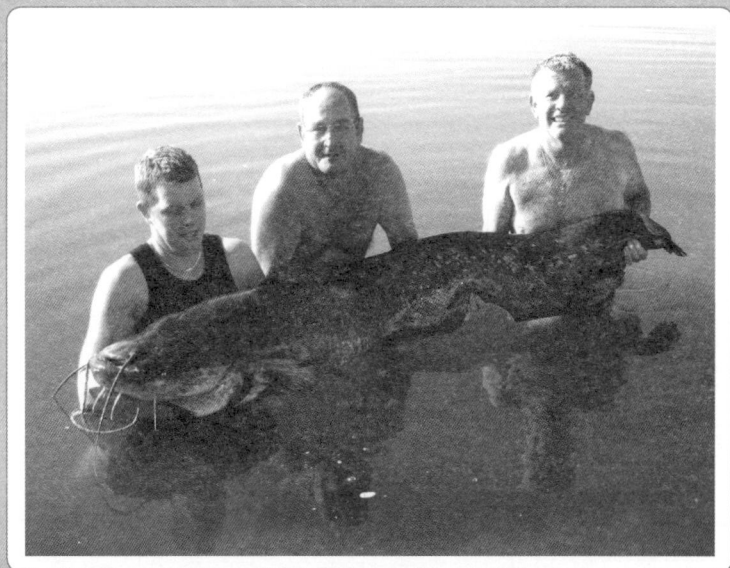

Robin Moyser (centre) with Andrew, his son, at the head of this 140lb beast

→ bottom. "The boat was set up to run the baits downstream, an easy way for beginners to learn. After just 15 minutes the first fish to take the bait started the reel clutch screaming as it plundered 80 metres of line before slowing down. It then took the angler 20 minutes to battle it to the boat. Resulting in a 90-pounder for my good friend Jasper the pint-pot Swede. Half an hour later a 115-pounder. Then the same again!"

There was no time to take in the peaceful surroundings, says Gary. "The tranquility was regularly shattered by burning reels and the mayhem that follows. At one point two fish were hooked simultaneously. What could be funnier? Watching, in the dark with a torch, one fish go one way and the other another, pulling the second angler around the boat. Now that was entertaining."

Gary often ties the right rig for a client until they've got the hang of it. "This has always been a necessary part of the job. It's my belief that patient encouragement invested in a client is usually rewarded with a boost in confidence on their part, when faced with the challenge of a new water. After all, this is the type of service a client should expect to receive after travelling a long way, and in return for their hard-earned cash.

"There is the exhilaration from the run, and the exhaustion from the battle, but for me it's the smile on the angler's face that stays in the mind for ever. I live for these moments."

For Gary, educating clients about the Ebro's superb aquatic environment and its inhabitants is all part of the holiday experience. "How much a catfish eats depends on the time of year, water temperature and river conditions. Floodwaters often lead fish into a feeding frenzy. Cold water slows them down. At prime feeding, a 100lb catfish can eat over 10 per cent of its body weight in one day!

"As the year progresses they change colour, from the dark silt tones where they've been laying up in winter to a brilliant mottled brown, with super cream shades running along the belly and underneath the tail."

Gary's multinational clientele broke the catfish record for the Lower Ebro three times in 2002 and 2003, with catches of 154.50lb,165lb and 167lb. Visit www.carpdreamfishing.com to find out more.

⬇ Heading Up The Ebro

Xerta (A: 20 minutes from Tortosa) has three more swims. Here the river widens out into a broad, beautiful valley. On its flanks are two irrigation canals which start at the Tiverneys l'Assut and run right to the sea. Their waters enable large-scale market gardening and gives the area its unique, green botanical feel.

Directions: drive 12km from Tortosa on the C12 (C230) road. It takes 20 minutes. Take the first signed right turn into Xerta, one kilometre along to the small town square. Turn right, go down 400 metres to the canal, turn left, go 200 metres to the canal bridge on your right. Cross over, park and have a drink. You've earned it. There is also a bus service, which takes 20 minutes from Tortosa. Cool off at the public shower by the bankside bar. If you miss the first turn-off, just head into the main street and turn right through the village, 800 metres down to the river. Do not take the new by-pass.

Swim 1 (B: 20 minutes): Your spot offers a beautiful view of the valley and hills beyond. It is to the left of the bay by the rocky outcrop. This offers the most fun and will fish all day. Carp run in at an average of 2.5kg. I used a heavy feeder rod with luncheon meat and loosebait little and often. I cast on to the shelf, use a running paternoster with a

Boat quay swims at Xerta on the River Ebro

quarter-ounce weight. If the weight keeps dropping, you have cast too far. The reach is 15 metres maximum. Bite detection is by touch; these are not subtle. The fish wait over the shelf for food to roll down from the shallow eddy.

Swim 2 (A: 20 minutes): This is a little further on from the bar, on the right of the boat quay. You will find this best from late afternoon till late evening and again in the mornings. Big carp, 10kg and up, will come in late to feed at this spot. I found float tackle with a heavier line to be the basic kit. Or paternoster with sweetcorn by the reeds, one or two rod lengths out. Loose feed little and often, or ring the changes with floated baits.

At night, I used a night light fixed to the rod tip for knock backs. At peak evening times hydro activity upstream around Riba-roja may cause the water level downstream to rise by half a metre in less than one hour. As a result, the carp will sometimes go into a feeding spree. With the warm water coming up past your shins in the darkness, this is not the time to panic. Take advantage of the situation. Bag up.

Swim 3 (B: 20 minutes): Located to the right of the quay at the village outflow pipe. Catfish will come up from beneath to eat hordes of mullet feeding off the effluent. You will observe intermittent swirls as the catfish take their dinner and you may see the odd carp hiding among the mullet.

Xerta is a safe and friendly village with one of the prettiest views of the Ebro. Visit the dam l'Assut 1km upstream. A good example of Moorish hydraulic engineering, it collects water for the two irrigation canals that supply the valley and Delta. There is a good restaurant directly opposite at Tiverneys. In the afternoon, go for a swim in Xerta's nice open-air pool, by the school.

Xerta's narrow streets are all laid out so they lead towards the river. This is the most efficient way of draining floodwater back to its source. If you think the village is a safe enough distance from the riverbank, check out the flood levels marked on the church wall in the small square opposite the bar. They go back to November 5, 1617. Powerful stuff. February 2003 saw the worst floods for 30 years.

For more information contact: Ayuntamiento, Pl. Major, 13, 43592 Xerta. Tel. 977 473 005: fax 977 473 014. Email: xerta@rhconsulting.es. www.xerta.altanet.org. www.ebre.com/xerta

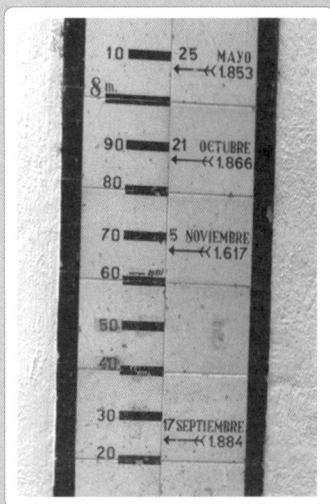

The author's father, Lawrie, beside the Limigraf on the church wall in the town square at Xerta, showing flood levels for the River Ebro going back centuries. The scale is at least 400m from the river and shows clearly the mighty power of the River Ebro

View of the River Ebro at Xerta, facing downstream

About 30 minutes' drive from Xerta, in an area of outstanding natural beauty, is the Horta de Sant Joan, which has a notable museum devoted to Picasso (tel. 977 435 005). Visiting here, Picasso's ideas about Cubism are said to have been influenced by the nearby Santa Barbara mountains' angular shape.

Benifallet (A: 35 minutes): Its location is right on the Ebro, set in a deep gorge with a great vista. Fish on the jetty in town or on the shingle bank nearby. Directions: just up from Xerta on the C12, over the bridge, or by the T301 up from Tiverneys. Hotel Pepo is a fishing friendly hotel at Benifallet. The hotel is located in a beautiful spot right on the Ebro and welcomes visiting anglers, with good storage facilities for all equipment and bait. Very reasonable rates — and they will never grow tired of your fishy stories.

Benifallet celebrates its Fiesta Mayor September 7-11. Visit the caves Coves de l'Aumediella, the Meravelles, Avenc del Sifo and Avenc del Catalanisme, open all year. Refreshing swims in the municipal pool. Ayuntamiento, Major,1, 43512 Benifallet. Tel. 977 462 005. Fax 977 462 289. www.benifallet.altanet.org

Beaches at Benifallet (C: 30 minutes): Be careful on approaching as the bank is steep and potholed. A point of interest here is an old, raised mound, site of the original donkey-powered pump which brought water up from the channel to the fields. Fight your way through the bushes and have a look. Insect repellent is advised. Directions: from Benifallet cross the new bridge over the Ebro. Head south for 1/3 km, and turn left. This track turns back on itself and runs parallel with the river. Arrive at the old ferry crossing (dead opposite the slipway at Benifallet). The ferry and winding gear remain and are worth investigating. Turn left and park under the trees. Through the vegetation to the right of a little brick pumping shed are located the beaches.

Landing a monster catfish

Catfish enthusiast Victor Edginton, from Deal in Kent, shares some of his extensive experience in fishing the Ebro:
"For many, landing a big catfish is the supreme achievement while on a Spanish fishing holiday. Fish from the bank or hire a local catfish guide. If you decide to use a guide, there is almost nothing for you to do apart from meeting his boat at the landing stage. You will be treated like

kings (and queens) for the day. Almost everything will be done for you. Tackle and bait are included in the price.

The guides will tell you where to meet them. This depends on where the cats are feeding at a given time of year. All you need to bring are soft-shoes, to protect the hull, a coolbox with lots of water, some food, hat protection. Additional clothing is optional.

> "The cat hits! All hell breaks loose. The novice angler panics, unable to decide how to handle it..."

The guide will bait up for you and put it in the water. Small carp and mullet are used as livebait. It may go against the grain, but this is catfishing. You then pay out the line to whatever distance you wish to fish at. It is then up to you whether you want to watch the float and pay attention – the correct way – or fix the rod into the rod holder, put the clicker on the reel and relax. Your guide may not like you doing this, as you may seem to be wasting his time. After all fishing is fishing.

When all the rods are in the water, the boat is slowly drifted along the channel with the aid of an electric trolling motor. On board is a sonar fish finder. Watching the screen is an eye-opener, as it picks up the location of many big carp that, frustratingly, you failed to catch the previous day.

The cat hits! All hell breaks loose. The novice angler panics, unable to decide how to handle a fish this big. Reassuringly, the guide is on hand so that you don't lose the skin on your thumb attempting to stop the 80lb braid from being stripped off the spool at the speed of light. You can hear the 80lb-class "up- tider" creaking as it bends to its full curve and all you can do is give the cat line when it wants it and gain line when the opportunity arises. At this point it's the fish or you. And in 80 degrees it's hot, hot fun. The fight lasts up to half an hour.

Finally, the huge head and body appear from the depths. The boat is leaning heavily towards the fish. Everyone has to lean to the opposite side. Sweat is pouring from your brow and your hands are slipping. But you have to stop the thing from diving under the keel or around the outboarders. At last it's lying still by the boatside. The guide gets both his gloved hands in its mouth and pulls. Welcome aboard! →

→ It slides on to the biggest weigh sling you have ever seen. Up go the scales. Now for the moment of truth: an 89lb albino. The fish of a lifetime. Photos follow and handshakes all around. After being held in the water for a minute to allow it to recover, the fish heads for the deep. A beer or two to celebrate as you shout: 'Ok. Let's do it again.'"

↓ Towards The Upper Ebro

Miravet (A: 1 hour): This is a beautiful town with solid town walls and a Templars' castle dating from the twelfth century. The name derives from "Murabit" meaning Islamic garden. The landscape is outstanding. Good all-round coarse fishing, roach and dace. Fish by the barge river crossing. Directions: go past Benifallet (19km to Miravet) on the C12, turn left on to TV3023, signposted into town.

Cross on the traditional ferry. It has no engine and is the last of its kind, just like the ferryman. Park near Arenal Square. Visit the old village (Cap de Vila) and view the dockyard and watermill. Miravet has great views of the Ebro and surrounding countryside. On August 10, 11 and 12,

PHOTO COURTESY OF PAUL DELANEY

Miravet Castle from the Río Ebro

El Setge de Miravet, a one- year siege which ended with the Templars' execution, is re-enacted at the castle, tickets at the tourist office, Tel: 977 40 76 26. In June take part in the Cherry Day festival, lots of cherry wine and dancing. Where to stay? La Casa Pequena (4 beds) y Grande (6 beds) self catering, with swimming pool, in Els Reguers near Tortosa, contact: Rob and Margaret Tel: 977 267382 Email: enquiries@ebrotours. co.uk or visit: www.ebrotours.co.uk

Móra d'Ebre (A: 50 minutes): Towards Móra the road passes through steep gorges with the Ebro hundreds of metres below. Plenty of fishing here and it is very popular. There are two swims north of town at the campsite, near the Caspender Restaurant. Directions: C230 north from Tortosa, following the river.

Pantà dels Guiamets (A: 1 hour 10 minutes): Free fishing in Tarragona province (barbel, carp, black bass, catfish, Iberian nase). Good depth, clean water. A do-gooder has introduced catfish to this water. Now there are lots of them – and in a short time there will be nothing else. A well-used lake. Directions: head east from Móra d'Ebre towards Reus on N420, exit southeast for Guiamets. From Reus, take the N420 west towards Móra d'Ebre. At exit for Masroig, turn off left instead for Guiamets. The water is towards east end of town.

Asco (A: 50 minutes): Area dominated by nuclear power station, due to be decommissioned in 2014. There's a good spot for crucian carp by the pontoon. Directions: turn down left by Coca Cola sign and go under a railway bridge in town. Locate the big catfish from your boat under the road bridge. The back eddy here is usually fishable when the river level is up and other swims are unfishable.

Flix (A: 1 hour): The small citadel town of Flix, about an hour's drive up the valley from Xerta and Tortosa, is set in an oxbow bend of the Ebro. The views along the route are impressive. The main road crosses the Ebro at a dam, below which there are many pools. From the turn-off, the road follows the river right around the town to the small car ferry. This will take you to the pegged swims on the opposite bank. From the bus stop you can cut through the town on foot instead of following the bend of the river.

Directions: take the C230. You can go by bus from Xerta or the terminal at Tortosa. The bus route is a stage (Viñaros to Tarragona) for the Tour of Spain bike race. The scale, severity and ruggedness of the landscape en route indicates how tough the competitors are.

Swim 1: Below the dam there are numerous pools to cast into. I found floated baits in the late afternoon were successful. Baiting up one swim with loose feed boilies (specialist carp angler bait) and freelining in is also worthwhile. Carp can be spotted from the elevated banks. Local day tickets can be purchased from Bar Catalunya in Flix for Swim 1 and from the tackle shop in Flix which looks like a toy shop from the street. They sell good value bags of boilies here at five euros a bag.

Swim 2: If your idea of a good day's fishing is to take a 50lb bag, this swim will keep you smiling. There are 10 pegs on the bank to the left of the ferry. As you cross over, take pleasure in the large schools of big carp. At the pegs nearest to the ferry, fish to the middle of the channel. As you progress to the farthest pegs 70 metres along the bank, fish to a maximum of 30 metres out, using heavy feeder tactics and groundbaiting. Pole fishing is recommended. Baits are luncheon meat, sweetcorn and commercial carp products. In fact the fish will eat anything.

I found the takes, while good, need a more assertive, fuller strike action than in other places. This is a prize-fighting arena and delicate, subtle bantamweight strikes will lead to disappointment. I have struck into some substantial fish, resulting in a slack parted line and a puzzled look. They may have been catfish. I now use a 15-kilo hook length and in any case the sport doesn't suffer. Once you strike into anything large, they go like a tractor and on occasions you end up with a straightened hook. Do make sure that your clutch is pre-adjusted.

Fishing is excellent dusk till dawn. There are lots of catfish at Flix. Use familiar methods and for a change cross back over the ferry and try the outflow pipe on the town side opposite the pegged swims.

Robin Smith, an angler based at Flix, comments on his experiences:

"Nine kilos is the biggest carp I have caught by the pegged swims and a three-kilo zander hooked on a 25cm lure! Fishing here is pretty consistent and I have found that pre-baiting is worthwhile. However this stretch becomes unfishable when the dam gates at Flix are opened. When the fish are hungry, the bites are stupendous as I found out to my cost, when £120-worth of rod and reel disappeared into the channel in the blink of an eye. For this reason braid line and bait runners are recommended."

Flix is surrounded on three sides by the bend of the Ebro, overlooked by the hilltop citadel. The town has large chemical and hydro plants. The ferry connects the farmers and their machinery in town to the outlying fields. This medieval commuting tradition survives from an age when the farming community sought refuge in numbers from nocturnal bandits. The morning rush hour is six tractors and three mopeds. Plus 40 goats, a hungry sheepdog and shepherd. They return for lunch and again at dusk. A cool beer for the bald ferryman will be appreciated. Stop press: on our last visit, his hair had grown to 1cm in length. This slow growth is definitely due to the high summer temperatures, 30 degrees Celsius, five degrees hotter than by the sea. For more information visit: www.cerespain.com/flix.html

Pantà de Riba-roja (A: 1 hour, 20 minutes): Big international competitions are held here. The Riba-roja dam is eight kilometres from town along a superbly finished road financed by the European Union. The locals fish for cats from inflatable lilos.

Above the dam, fish at the reservoir. Below the dam, the campsite side is day ticket, the other side is free. Do the fish care? The carp below the dam are usually bigger and it's ok to drive down the track from the kilometre marker as long as the weather's good. When it rains, a four-wheel-drive is required.

Catfishing here is very good and there are large bags of carp. The water is exceptionally clear — you can see down six or seven metres. Likewise the fish can spot you! There is a tackle shop in town that sells good tackle and carp baits.

Directions: At Flix turn left for Riba-roja, just before you cross over the dam, on T741. For tickets: Hotel Pepito, tel: 977 416 526; Bar la Granga, tel: 977 416 037; Bar la Plaça, tel: 973 138 203, 5km further along from the campsite, at Badia Tucana, a small inlet for boat hire and tourism. www.riba- roja.altanet.org Club de Pesca Bass Catalunya, Embalse de Riba-roja, Fayón, www.basscatalunya.com

Coto de Matarranya (C: 1 hour, 15min): Riu Matarranya, near La Pobla de Massaluca. Carp and catfish. The river is a feeder to the Riba-roja reservoir. Day ticket. Tel: 977 416 001. Directions: from Flix go west via Riba-roja, T741, TV7411, TV7231. From Gandesa go north TV7231. To locate the water, follow the track east out of town for a few kms.

Mequinenza (A: 3 hours): Over-rated, Bavarian in flavour, very expensive, but all the facilities. Very good camping, toilets, showers, bar restaurant. Locals sometimes fish for catfish in two-man canoes. Occupying a superb position, Mequinenza is strategically located at the confluence of two big rivers, the Ebro and the Segre. A large castle built by the Moors stands 130 metres above the Ebro. Directions: located north of Riba-roja. From Flix, take roads T741,TV7411, TV7231 to Fayón, then the A1411 into town.

In some locations here you will need an Aragón government licence (e.g. for the river Segre west bank). Purchase one in any of the bars of Granja d'Escarp or the tackle shop in Mequinenza, where you can also buy angling insurance (a mandatory purchase). The police here are officious. No nightfishing after midnight. Also try at Escatrón, Chiprana and Fayón. Further information: S.D.P. El Siluro, Ctra. de Fraga, s/n, 50170 Mequinenza. Tel: 976 465134.

Embalse de Caspe (C: 3 hours): Part of a vast lake system above the Mequinenza dam. Crystal clear water. "Like fishing in heaven," say some anglers. There is an annual international black bass festival, a no-holds-barred type of event. Popular with Americans, it features big powerboats and high-speed trotting. Good barbel and huge carp here, but few bother with them. Directions: Take the C12 up towards Benifallet, just before the bridge turn left to Gandesa on the C43. Then

PHOTO COURTESY OF BEACHCOMBER JOHN, MOJÁCAR ANGLING CLUB

Embalse de Caspe – "Fishing in Heaven"

make for Maella, first on the N420, then the C221. The C221 continues to Caspe. From Mequinenza, take the N211 southwest to Caspe.

Lake Caspe Camping is right on the water. Two-thirds of way on N211from Mequinenza to Caspe turn right. Signposted. Nice swimming pool and regional angling licences sold on site. Look out for wild boar, and red deer taking a drink. Egyptian vultures swoop to take fish. To the north is Los Monegros, a semi- desert, a good place to camp during the summer. Further information: Lake Caspe Camping, Ctra. N211 km286.7, 50700 Caspe. Tel: 976 632 486 correo@lakecaspe.com

River Segre (B: 3 hours): Famous for pike. Good barbel and roach. The Segre is a feeder to the Ebro. This area remains untainted by the problems facing the Ebro, so may well be your cup of tea. Directions: Fish from Mequinenza upriver (N211), to Granja d'Escarp. Or take the C12 to above Lleida. The east bank requires the Catalan regional licence. The west bank is in Aragón so you will need a regional licence for that region. Both licences can be purchased from the tackle shop in Mequinenza or at the bars at Granja d'Escarp. Eel baiting on the Catalan side is prohibited. For more information on fishing in this area, contact Domingo Artiques of the Lleida Angling Club, Hostal Catalunya, Ponts (Lleida). Tel: 973 460 210/460 842. Tino@trends-online.com

John Wrenn, a member of the Mojácar Angling Club, describes the club's successful trips to the River Ebro:

When we visited in October and early November, 2005, the main river around Mequinenza was very difficult to fish, with lots of floating weed. Siluro catfish of around 160lb were being caught daily and carp to 36lb. We fished a few venues including the main river and Caspe. We also tried fishing the small slow-running river at Alcañiz and the larger faster-running one at Fraga, but all without success. Many Germans, Dutch, French and others turn up with fish from their own countries for livebaiting. This is how it is thought rudd, roach and bleak have arrived.

The future could see some new European roach records as we caught only three but they were 3/4lb to 1.1lb each. No doubt before long before they will be feeding on 20mm halibut pellets — then we'll see some growth.

Our favourite spot was the Embalse de Riba-roja. Other than black →

→ bass and zander fishermen out in boats, there were few others, even at weekends. Where we fished, swims are easily accessed, with car parking on the spot. The water is about two metres below and the water's edge reached by climbing down rocks. The flooded river, usually without a flow, is full of snags, mainly a ledge of what is believed to be big rocks, and fish bolt into these. There are also dead trees, probably flooded orchards, to get snagged on or for fish to transfer their hooks to.

The water deepens quickly to four metres at six metres out. The depth stays roughly the same until the aforementioned ledge 30 to 40 metres out. I believe there are more ledges before the original river-bed further out where, I'm told, the siluro catfish hole up and also where the big carp go during the colder months.

A boat is needed to get out to this area. Why would you want to fish there? Because there are big fish to be caught and nobody else fishes the area. Without leaving tackle out all night as many anglers do, we are still pretty certain of finding our pre-baited swims available to us the following morning. I recommend four-metre, 3lb-test curve carp rods and heavy-duty baitrunner/big pit reels with 250 metres of 15lb line. Bring twice what you think you will need in end tackle — although

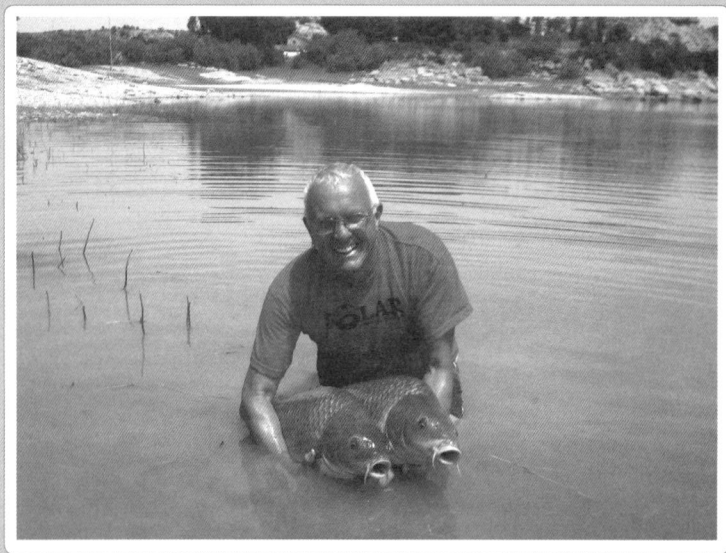

PHOTO COURTESY OF BEACHCOMBER JOHN, MOJACAR ANGLING CLUB

Fishing the Ebro – John Wrenn with a 30lb and 24lb double hook up caught near Caspe

there are three tackle shops in Mequinenza, good end tackle is limited. Secondly, don't go far from your rods, as the fish will be in snags before you pick them up. We DIY'd our Ebro fishing, but next time some of us intend using a guide for a day. I would advise others to do so as, no matter how experienced a fisherman is in this field in the UK, fishing the Ebro is different. And what you learn in one day will be useful for the rest of the trip.

⬇ From Zaragoza to Mequinenza

For centuries this stretch has attracted anglers. Ask Sancho Panza. Miguel de Cervantes in his famous book Don Quixote de La Mancha wrote how "Don Quixote and Sancho reached the river Ebro, and the sight of it was a great delight to Don Quixote as he contemplated the charms of its banks, the clearness of its stream, the gentleness of its current and the abundance of its crystal waters". Sancho informed the knight that "they catch the best shad in the world here".

Don Quixote didn't need a licence, but you do — purchase your Aragón licence at: Instituto Aragonés Gestión Medio Ambiental, Edificio Trovador, Plaza Antonio Beltrán Martínez,1-5A Planta, 5002 Zaragoza. Tel. 976 715 181; or Federación Aragonesa de Pesca, Padre Marcellán, 15, 50015 Zaragoza. Tel. 976 730 827. Fax. 976 735 632. Email fapyc@fapvc.org. www.fapyc.org

Zaragoza can be reached by direct trains and buses from Barcelona or by the A2 autoroute.

Follow the advice of Norman Smith, an old hand at fishing the waters of Spain, and "try the River Ebro above the uppermost road bridge in the city of Zaragoza at the Playa de los Angeles public park. This area is just stuffed with carp up to low doubles with a few 20s if you are lucky and some elusive big 'uns — barbel, occasionally, catfish and pike. The channel consists of a gradually sloping gravel bank where the water slowly increases in depth until the far side is reached, at a distance of 50 metres. Cast here for the best results. However, when the water level is up, it is necessary to fish from the far bank."

From Zaragoza take the NII east through Nuez de Ebro town centre, then over the A2 *autovía* (motorway) to the **Presa de Pina**. To the right, near a power station, are a small pinewood and date palms, beyond which is a small fishing area with gentle current. Bleak, common barbel, carp and some medium-sized catfish occupy this zone. Sweetcorn is good for carp. Downstream from the power station, there is a poplar grove with good shade and easy access for cars. The bankside is quite wide, although the current after the small dam increases.

Take the NII and turn off for **Pina de Ebro**. At the bridge, turn right, drive about 6km, always following the course of the Ebro. The water is a greenish colour and good for carp, bleak, barbel and a few catfish. Return and take the N232 and head towards Quinto de Ebro.

Along this route are different sections: fast current, backwaters, meanders, and reed banks. Carp predominate and, in the faster current, catfish and barbel, especially in the first section up to an old water station. From here downstream, it's a little calmer. Choose your swim in the gaps between the vegetation.

The next destination is **Quinto** which has some good-size perch in addition to the species already mentioned. Best swims are at the meanders and fig groves near town. Bass anglers will enjoy this area, because it is completely different from the main channel of the Ebro.

Best swims in Quinto are at the meanders and fig groves near town. Bass anglers will enjoy ths area, as it's completely different from the main channel of the Ebro

Leaving Quinto, take the N232 towards Alcañiz but just outside town turn left towards La Zaida, Sástago and Escatrón. Towards La Zaida (15 km away), the current is strong and dark in colour. From La Zaida, head towards Sástago for about 5km, then turn towards the small town of **Cinco Olivas**. Here there are a dam, holes, fast water and meanders. This is a pretty stretch but access is difficult.

From Sástago, go east across the Ebro bridge. Here the fishing changes. Now it's catfish and zander. Follow the road towards Escatrón road. Either turn left towards the Monasterio de Rueda a little before the Escatrón bridge, or pass over the bridge and go left along a track, the Camino del Embarcadero. By following either of these country roads, you will happen upon good-size zander and catfish.

From Escatrón towards Chiprana the banks get wider and more

accessible. Catfish is the dominant species here. About 3km before Chiprana a bridge crosses the first arm of the **Mequinenza reservoir** (Pantà de Mequinensa, on Catalan maps), aka El Mar de Aragón. There are a lot of carp, catfish and zander around the village of Regallo.

Numerous routes lead to the reservoir and the catfish sport becomes prolific according to the time of the year. Bottle rigs are prohibited and it's most usual to bait up with alburno (bleak), live or dead bait. Select different arms and points around the reservoir depending on the water level.

The Mequinenza reservoir is free fishing when in possession of the Aragón licence. Large catfish fall to crankbait lures. Ondulants, spoons and vinyls mounted in a jig will catch large pike. Carp from this zone up to Chacón Viejo, near Caspe. Boat fishing is permitted from Regallo. The Chiprana zone gets tricky because the shallow depth during summer below Chiprana endangers boat traffic. From a gravel bar on a bend in the river to Chacón, navigation is safer although the water remains cloudy.

↓ Costa Brava-Girona

The locations mentioned, though only a short journey time from the popular Costa Brava resorts, offer a real taste of the Spanish fishing experience. The lakes and rivers just inland reveal much more. Most waters are positively under- fished.

Carp and barbel remain the dominant species on the rivers Ter, Fluvial and Tordera. Lago Banyoles, for example, has a well-earned reputation for offering some great carp angling. It's less than one hour's drive from the resort of Estartit on the Costa Brava.

The Ter passes through the region of Ripolles and Osona before dissipating in the marshes at the foot of Montseny. Besalú and Beget have fine medieval bridges. To the west at Camprodon the valley is wide and fertile. Here the Pont Nou, built in the 12th century, gives access to the Cardagne valley.

Where do I buy my angling licence?
Sección Territorial para la Conservación de la Naturaleza, Avda. de San Francisco, 29, 17001 Girona. Tel: 972 212 400. Fax: 972 209 413. Email: acros/o@gencat.net. www.gencat.net/darp

Where do I get a boat licence?

Agencia Catalana de l'Aigua, C/Ciutadans, 11, 17004 Girona. Tel: 972 213 812. Fax: 972 213 727. Angling information: Federació Catalana de Pesca Esportiva, Bejar, 59 baixos, 08014 Barcelona. Tel: 932 893 300. Fax: 932 890 552. www.fcpeic.com Email: fedecatpesca@fcpceic.com

Want to combine your holiday on the coast with a day or two fishing?

Some suggestions: **Embassament Vallforners** (Embalse de Vallfornés), Besos river, half an hour from Arenys de Mar, day ticket (carp and trout). Buy tickets at: Restaurant Can Carriga, Sant Muc, 8, Cánoves, tel: 938 710 047; Amor Sports, Rec, 3, Granollers, tel: 938 790 995. Buy your tackle and bait here. Directions: from Barcelona east C33, C35, exit north BV5108 for Cánoves. From Arenys, C61 north, C35 west, then north BV5107 for Cánoves.

Coto de Valors, Riera Santa Coloma, half an hour from Lloret de Mar, day ticket (carp, trout). Fish from the Pont Nou d'en Martorell to the Pont de la Coebera. For tickets: Bar Tramuntana, Verge María, 11, Sta. Coloma de Farners, tel: 972 840 237. Directions: from Lloret north on C63 to Santa Coloma. From Girona south on A7/E15, west C25 to Santa Coloma.

> Estany de Banyoles is Catalonia's only natural lake. Abundant wildlife, including coots, herons, whistling ducks and the plumed grebe

Estany de Banyoles, free fishing (carp and barbel). Some whoppers! Catalonia's only natural lake. Abundant wildlife, including coots, small herons, whistling ducks and the plumed grebe. The lake is 2km in length, average depth 15 metres, 46 metres maximum. Continually incoming groundwater accounts for 80 per cent of the lake's total inflow. Directions: northwest of Girona on C66.

This is the first water in Catalonia to stock black bass. It has a prolific history of introductions and is recognised as a scientific control on the effects of introduced fish species on native stocks. Tench, carp, catfish, pumpkinseed, brown and rainbow trout, pike, perch, zander and crucian have all been introduced. Barbel and eels are native species. The 1992 Olympic rowing events were held on this water.

Contestants in an annual fishing contest set off from the town hall followed by a band playing arias. They arrive, a little worse for wear, at a pond called l'Estanyol de Vilar, near the main lake.

Banyoles is a pleasant family town. The very popular big festa of the year is held on the third Sunday in October. Information from Turismo, tel: 972 575 573, Passeig de la Industria, 25. You can camp at El Lac, tel: 972 570 305, towards the town of Porqures on south shore. Hotels are cheaper in Girona.

Riu El Terri, Estany de Banyoles, day ticket (carp). There are three stretches for fishing. Buy your tickets at: Bar la Carpa (they should know where the fish are), at Passeig Darder, 10, Banyoles, tel: 972 582 825. Directions: half an hour s drive north of Girona, N11, C66, northwest.

Boadella I, Riu Muga, Boadella d'Empordá, 40 minutes from Roses, day ticket (carp, barbel, perch and zander). Fish from Les Escaules sluice gate to the Boadella d'Empordá lock. Tickets may be purchased from Armería Romero, Figueres, tel: 972 500 557, and at the Café del Pont, Pont de Molins, tel: 972 528 345. Zander were introduced to the Embalse Boadella, near Figueres, as a sporting fish in the 1980s, probably from Switzerland, to attract French and German tourists. It rapidly spread to the Mequinenza and Caspe reservoirs on the Río Ebro. Then to the Río Segre (Lleida). Directions: from Figueres go north on N11 for a few km, then exit west GIV5041, 8 km to les Escaules. Boadella is a little further up the valley.

Boadella II, Riu Muga, Sant Lorenc, an hour from l'Escala, day ticket (carp, zander, black bass). Fish from the Presa de Boadella to the bridge at the entrance to Sant Lorenç (Muga), and to the Resclosa de Moli Masarell (Arnera). Purchase tickets at: Fonda llossa, Darnius, tel: 972 535 352; Café del Pont, Pont de Molins, tel: 972 528 345; Botiga Tots Els Articles, St. Lorenç de la Muga, tel: 972 535 352. Directions: from Figueres go north on N11 for 5 km then exit west, GIP5107 through Pont Molins, west on GI510 another 15 km to Sant Llorenç de la Muga.

Riu Ter and Riu Onyar, Girona, half hour from: l'Estartit, day ticket (carp). Fish all along the Riu Ter from the Pont de Fontajau just west of the rivers' confluence 3km, up to Sarrià at the Fábrica Torras (factory tower) of Sarria de Ter, left bank, and the incinerator of Campdora. Fish the Riu Onyar from the confluence with the Ter to the bridge Pont de Pedra at Girona. For tickets: Pesca d'Or, Ctra N11 km 722, Sant Julia de Ramis, tel: 972 172 717; Bar Restaurant La Pastora, Ctra França, s/n Sarrià de Ter, tel: 972 170 744; Armería Escatidor, C/Jaume 1, 32,

> **Beget and Riera de Beget offer free fishing for the connoisseur. This is clear water angling in authentic mountain country**

Girona, tel: 972 214 980. Directions: the Riu Ter runs alongside the N11a from Girona up to Sarrià.

Up in the Pyrenees towards the French border, **Beget and Riera de Beget** offer free fishing for the connoisseur (mountain barbel). Clear water angling in authentic mountain country. Access can be problematic. Leave your car in town, then go by foot. Friendly locals at the town bar will tell you what to do. Directions: Go northwest from Girona C66, N260, to Olot. Then follow the Ter up the valley past Camprodon C26, C38. Turn right on to GIV5223 (this is a narrow road) to Beget, 12 km. Where to stay? At the nearby mountain resort of Camprodon. Can Ganasi, C/Josep Morera 11, is just off the Plaza de España. Try ringing in advance, tel: 972 740 134.

Sant Hipolit de Voltrega, Riu Ter, day ticket (carp). Fish from the Pont de la Mina del Pla de Torroella to the Resclosa Paratl. For tickets: Restaurant Cal Peyu, C17, km 77 de Maises de Voltrega, tel: 938 570 491. Directions: from Girona A7/E15 south, C25 west, N152 north from Vic to St. Hipolit de Voltrega.

Manlleu, Riu Ter, day ticket (carp). Fish from the Pont de Plana de Coll to the Pont de la Mina del Pla de Torroella. For tickets: La Canya, Montseney, 65, Manlleu, tel: 938 512 069; Business Café, C/Tarragona, 50, Manlleu, tel: 938 511 919. Directions: from Girona A7/E15 south, C25 west, north from Vic, B522 to Manlleu.

Roda de Ter, Riu Ter, day ticket (carp). Fish from the Torrent de les Valls to the Pont de Plans del Coll. Tickets: Bar Cal Rabada, Ctra, de Barcelona, 12 Roda de Ter, tel: 938 500 081. Directions: from Girona A7/E15 south, C25 west, north from Vic, BV5222 to Roda.

Santa María de Corco, Riu Ter, day ticket (carp). Fish from the Presa de Pantà de Sau to the Torrent de les Valls. Tickets: Snack Bar Rovi, Ctra. Sant Bartomeu, 6, Santa María de Corco, tel: 938 568 046. Directions: from Girona A7/E15 south, C25 west, northeast from Vic, C153 to Corco. Torello, Riu Ter, day ticket (carp). Fish from: the Resclosa Parato, Espademaia de Baix (lower esplanade) to the Pont de Borgunya. For tickets: Restaurant Ges, 3 de Torello, Ter, tel: 935 805 071. Directions: Girona A7/E15 south, C25 west, north from Vic, C17/N152, C37 to Torello.

↓ Barcelona

The Llobregat river valley provides a well-stocked backdrop for Barcelona's large angling community. Excellent fishing begins just to the north, near Terrassa. The river flows through some great scenery from the rock at Montserrat to beyond Berga, 90km to the north. The drive up the valley is pleasant and there's a carefree atmosphere in the pretty villages along the way. The river, 170km in length, is divided into four regions, Berueda, Baixes, Baix Llobregat and the river basin. Its source is in the Pla de Rus and Pla d'Anyella mountains. It rises on the south slope of the Sur del Montmell, at 1,295 metres above sea-level, near the town of Castellar de n'Hug.

The Llobregat's name is derived from the Roman word Rubricatus. In the 19th century the area was heavily industrialised and the Llobregat became a working river. Today its many water mills are a feature of the area's industrial heritage. Following the valley from east to west, it receives the waters of L'Aritja. At Guardiola de Bergada, it turns south, shortly being joined by the Bastareny. The river is flanked by the Serra de Catallares on its east bank and by the Serra d'Ensija, Los Rasos de Peguera and Serra de Queralt on the west. Many waters are day ticket and cost as little as three euros. Income generated keeps the environment clean. Prices remain low compared to the UK. All in all, this entire region is great value for money.

Where do I buy my angling licence?
Consejería de Medio Ambiente, Avda. Diagonal, 523/525, 08029 Barcelona. Tel: 935 674 200. Also try the Consejería de Agricultura, Ganadería y Pesca de la Generalitat de Catalunya, Córcega, 329 - planta 5, 08037 Barcelona. Tel: 932 377 862. This river authority covers the Llobregat-Foix, Tordera-Besos rivers.

Need a boat licence?
Agencia Catalana de l'Aigua, Provença, 204-208, 08036 Barcelona. Tel: 935 672 800. Fax: 935 672 780. More information: Club Pesca Bass Catalunya, Sant Jaume, 102, 08400 Granollers. Tel: 938 790 995, 934 263 422. Email: info@basscatalunya.com

All directions given are for a start from Barcelona unless otherwise stated.

Pantà de Reixach, Riu Gavarresa, free fishing (carp). This is a small, shallow lake, but it offers quite a pleasant day out. Directions: northeast on A17, C17 past Granollers. Just before Vic go west, C25D, then west, C154 towards Prats de Llucanes. At Olost de Llucanes, go right for al Cruce de Reixach, towards Santa Creu de Jutglars, BV4405.

Pantà de Sau, Riu Tordera, free fishing and day ticket (carp, trout, black bass, bleak, and catfish). Popular deep-water dam in a beautiful setting. It's an easy fish and an ideal spot for beginners and the family. There are a lot of smaller carp, easily caught, to 1-3kg. Big bags are common, averaging 15kg and up to 25kg. On May 23, 2000, 60 carp were landed in just five hours. Baits to use are maggots and sweetcorn. Smaller catfish are the order of the day. A bigger one, to 14kg, was caught near Sau on August 8, 2002. For bass, try spinning with a shallow shad Rapala or a green Rapala. For trout try the bell tower. Day tickets can be obtained at the bar-restaurant to the right, shortly before the dam wall. Typically, the water can be 35 to 45 per cent full. These figures are par for the course in this region, but don't let that put you off going as the fishing is unaffected.

Directions: from Barcelona go north A17, C17 to Vic. Take ring road clockwise round Vic and exit southeast, C25 (easy route east, 20 km from Vic). Exit east, N414d east past Vilanova de Sau. To Sant Roma de Sau. Go over dam wall, on this road, to the Hotel Casa de Campo. This is next to the water. From: Girona A7 south, C25 west to Vic.

> **→ Top Tip:** During the summer, water levels everywhere will be at their lowest. Don't be put off. Catch the big carp by casting to them at the middle of the water, at its deepest. If the lake is full of small carp, crayfish and terrapins, simply use a harder, bigger bait to deter them.

Coto de Abrera, Riu Llobregat, day ticket (carp). Fish from the outlet (*desembocadura*) of Riera Morra to the *desembocadura* Riera Magorola. Stretch length is 5km. For tickets in Abrera go to Bar Bodega Rambla, Rbla Torrent, 4, tel: 937 001 006; Bar Rosales; Bar Mesón Sta. Cruz: Llobregat, 7; Restaurant la Chopera, Ctra. Vella Olesa, tel: 937 700 997. Directions: go northwest, N11, C1414, exit at Abrera.

Coto de Moli de Can Sedo, Riu Llobregat, day ticket (carp and some barbel). Fish from the Riera Margarola, right bank, and at the Roca (cliff) de la Mona (left bank) to the Cairat weir (*resclosa*). The *tramo* (fishing stretch) is 8km long. A lot of small fish. Carp will average 2kg. For tickets: Bar Granja Joan, Calveri, 54, Olesa de Montserrat, tel: 937 786

091. Directions: north N11, exit at Olesa de Montserrat. River is on left, west of town. Or north C16, exit west, junction 11, B121, B120.

Coto de Castellbell i El Vilar, Riu Llobregat, day ticket (good size barbel and carp). Fish from the sluice gate of Castellbell i El Vilar to the Resclosa de Sant Vincen (Serramalera) left bank. Length is 2km. A family spot set in a lovely woodland location. For tickets go to Café Bures, C/Bures, 22, Castellbell i El Vilar, tel: 938 340 206. Useful information: Egara fishing club in Terrassa (Barcelona) and Dom Bosco, Roca i Roca, 198 (esquina Proenza), 08226 Terrassa, tel: 937 319 212. Directions: north, C16, exit after junction 12, west for Castellbell. The river is on left side of town.

Coto de Castellgalí, at the confluence of Llobregat and Cardener rivers, day ticket (carp). For tickets: Bar La Carpa, Avda. Montserrat, s/n, Castellgallí, tel: 938 332 104. Directions: N11 north, C55 up to Castellgalí. Exit here, the river is to right of main road. Don't go left into town.

Coto de St. Joan de Vilatorrad, Riu Cardener, day ticket (carp, barbel and bleak). Fish from the Resclosa Pirelli to the Pont Ctra Callus, St. Mateu de Bages. The fishing stretch is 7km in length. Buy tickets at Local Social Joanenca de Pesca, St. Isidre, 24 St. Joan de Vilatorrado, tel: 938 764 866. Directions: go north E9, exit at Manresa. C37, C25 to Vilatorrado. Then to Sant Joan de Torrvell, N141.

Pantà de Can Macia, Odena, free fishing (carp, bleak, crucian, and black bass). 3-4 metres deep, some weed. Best spots are at the bridge section and around town. Recommended local baits are maggots and worms. Directions: go northwest, N11 to Igualada. Exit here north C37. Halfway to Odena, exit at las Caves Boligas. After the straight the road curves to the right. In a short while you will see the small reservoir.

Coto de Suria, Riu Cardener, day ticket: (carp). Fish from the Resclosa de la Fábrica Nova (sluice gate at the new factory) to the Cementiri (cemetery) Valis Torruella. 11km in length. Carp to 10kg. A lot of barbel. Very pretty. Good spot for the family, with a barbecue area. It costs 10 euros to fish, rather expensive for Spain, but the results are good. For tickets go in Suria to: Agrupacio de Pescadors, tel: 938 696 258; Bar Capri, Ctra. Baisareny, 1, tel: 938 696 258; Bar Cai Fusteret, Angel Guimera, 29, tel: 938 696 761. Directions: go north E9, exit at Manresa, C55 north, just past Suria, north, in direction of Cardona.

Coto de Els Bacus, Riu Llobregat, day ticket (carp, some barbel and catfish, a lot of bleak). Fish from the weir (*resclosa cremallera*) of Montserrat to the TM Castellbell i El Vilar amb Monistrol. Length is 1km. For tickets: Bar Terrassa, Rambla Egara, 256, Terrassa, tel: 937 865 044. Directions: north, C58, exit just south of Terrassa, west to Can Panellada (BP.1505). River is west of here.

Coto de Can Xiviro, Riu Llobregat, day ticket (carp). Fish from beginning to end of the municipal boundaries of Castellbell i El Vilar. *Tramo* (fishing stretch) is 3km in length. Tickets at Castellbell: Llar d'Avis, Joaquín Boras, 38, tel: 938 340 292; Bar la Bauma, tel: 938 282 281; Restaurant La Torra, tel: 938 340 333. Café Bures, tel: 938 340 206. Directions: north C16, exit junction 12 west, C58 north for Castellbell i El Vilar.

Coto de Monistrol de Montserrat, Riu Llobregat, day ticket (carp). Fish from the Pont de l'Arei to the Bacus dam or sluice. Fishing stretch length is 3 km. For tickets: Bar la Cantonado, Balmes, 41, Monistrol, tel: 938 350 211. Directions: north C16, junction 12, exit west, C58 to El Borras. South C55 to Monistrol de Montserrat. You can't miss it. River is to right of town. Where to stay? Hotel Abat Cisneros, Plaça del Monestir, tel: 938 777 701; fax: 938 284 006. They have cheaper accommodation at Hotel-Residencia Monestir, same telephone numbers. Camping, beyond the Sant Joan funicular, is well signposted, tel: 938 350 251. Warning: avoid April 27 and September 8 at all costs and probably a week either side unless you are a Catholic pilgrim.

> In Coto de Monistrol de Montserrat, avoid April 27 and September 8 at all costs and probably a week either side unless you are a Catholic pilgrim

Coto de El Cairat, Riu Llobregat, day ticket (carp). Fish from Mur Resclosa de Cairat to the Pont Aeri de Montserrat. Length is 2km. For tickets: Bar Industria, Industria, 7, Martorell, tel: 937 740 328. Directions: north N11, C55, towards Monistrol de Montserrat. Then towards Cairat. Coto de Can Serra, Riu Llobregat, day ticket (barbel, tench, bleak and carp). Fish from the Presa de Can Serra to the Presa de Can Belet. *Tramo* (fishing stretch) length is 1.3km. For tickets, Bar Coro, Lobregat, 12, St. Vicenç, tel: 938 334 423. Directions go north, C16. Before Manresa, exit at junction 13, Sant Vicenç de Castellet. River is at left side of town.

Coto de St. Vicenç de Castellet, Riu Llobregat, day ticket (carp). Fish from Presa Can Balet to the Punt FFCC Generalitat Sant Jaume. Fishing stretch 3km long. This is a very accessible spot. Bags of carp up to 20kg have been landed. Baits popular here include maggots. The fishing is free from the bridge to Manresa highway. For tickets: Bar Bonachera, Gran, 52, at St. Vincenc, tel: 938 334 165. Directions: go north, C16. Before Manresa, exit at junction 13, Sant Vincenc de Castellet. River is at left side of town.

Palleja, Riu Llobregat, free fishing (carp, barbel, pumpkinseed, eels and alets). Deep and calm river, clean banks. Directions: drive northwest, A2, N11, exit at Sant Vincenc, N11a, north to Palleja. There are three ways to access the river, all to east of town.

Coto de El Pont de Vilomara, Riu Llobregat, day ticket (carp). Fish from the confluence of the Riera de Sant Esleve to the Resclosa dels Carburs (sluice gate). *Tramo* (fishing stretch) length is 3.5km. For tickets: Bar Chiringuito, Jesus, 110, Pont de Vilomara, tel: 938 318 082. Directions: go north, C16. Before Manresa, exit east at junction 14. Go south, BV.1229 to El Pont de Vilomara.

Coto de Manresa, Riu Cardener, day ticket (carp). Length is 9km. For tickets: Pesca Parera, Urgell, 11, Manresa, tel: 938 723 103. Directions: go north E9, exit at Manresa. Go south towards suburb of Santa Batel.

Buy your angling licence at: Dept d'Agricultura y Pesca, Sant Joan d'en Coll, 9, 08240 Manresa (Bages). Tel. 938 736 400. Fax. 938 733 212. ajescca@gencat.net

Coto de St. Benet de Bages, Riu Llobregat, day ticket (carp). Fish from the Aiguabarreig (confluence) Riera de Mura, to the Fábrica de Sant Benet. For tickets: Social UPE Sabadell, Fuerteventura, 26, Sabadell, tel: 937 263 049; Bar Stop, Ctra. De Vic, 94, St. Frutos de Bages, tel: 938 760 952. Directions: north C16, just past Manresa, exit 16, east towards Navarcles C1411. River is nearby at Bages.

Coto de Pantà de la Baells, Riu Llobregat, *coto especial* (trout and pike). A big popular lake. Take lots of water. If you don't have a brolly, wear a protective hat. Good in winter for pike — they eat a lot of trout. Catfish and black bass make an appearance. For tickets: Bar Pi Negre, Cercs, tel: 938 248 611; Bar Comellas, Vilada, tel: 938 238 154; Restaurant Rovello, Cr. de Berga, 18, Cal Rosal (Olva), N1411, tel: 938 221 406. The motorboats annoy everyone at the weekends. Directions:

north C16 past Manresa, north to Berga. Two options: C16 north to Cercs (La Rodonella), or C26, east towards Vilada. The road goes over the water.

Balsareny, Riu Llobregat, day ticket (carp and trout). Fish from El Lledo de Sobreroca to Vilafruna. For tickets: Guarda de la Zpc, Travessera, 49, Balsareny, tel: 938 396 510. Directions: C16/C1411 north of Manresa. Llac de Navarcles, Riu Calders, day ticket: (carp). For tickets: Bar Sport Avda. Piscines I Esports, 17 Navarcles, tel: 93 827 0521. Directions: east of Manresa, E9/C16, J16 for Navarcles.

Narvarclina de Pesca, Riu Llobregat, day ticket (carp). Fish from: the Monestir Sant Benet to the Pont Cabrianes. Tickets and directions: same as as Llac de Navarcles.

Cornet-Dosrius-Llobregat, Llobregat and Cardener rivers, day ticket (carp). Fish from Resclosa Castellgalí (Cardener) to the Riera Cornet, and from Resclosa Dosrius (Llobregat) to the Pont Ferro. For tickets: Restaurant Braseria Can Sebas, Anselm Calve, 2, Castellgalí, tel: 938 330 622. Directions: Barcelona north C55 just south of Manresa. L'Empalma, Riu Llobregat, day ticket (carp and trout). Fish from the Palanca dels Curtais to the Antiga Resclosa de Cal Caseta, Font del Roser. For tickets, in Pobla de Lillet: Bar Ca l'Angel, tel: 938 236 436; Bar Xesc, tel: 938 236 522; Restaurant El Verger, tel: 938 380 294; Bar Fior de Neu, tel: 938 236 201. Directions: E9/C16/C1411 north, past Berga, east B402, Pobla.

Torrent de Solls, Torrent de la Collada de Montcius, Font del Bisbe, day ticket (carp, trout). Fish from the Aiguabarreig amb l'Arija (Teulana) to the Aiguamolla de Naixement (Sta. Eugenia de les Solls). Tickets: in Pobla de Lillet, as for L'Empalma. Directions: as for L'Empalma.

Cardener, Cardener 2, day ticket (carp). Fish from the Gual (Vado) de Valideperas, la Cort to the Reslosa del Paperer. For tickets: Bar Centro, Pl. de la Fira, 21, Cardona, tel: 938 691 135. Directions: C16 north Manresa. C55 northwest, Cardona.

Cuenca del Llobregat, El Llobregat, free fishing. Fish from the bridge at the crossing of BV4022 with C1411, just north of Cercs (Berga), to the dam on the industrial canal at Collet. Directions: drive up the valley, past Berga.

⬇ Costa Dorada

Licences: Consejería de Medio Ambiente, Cardenal Vidali Barraquer, 12-14, Tarragona. Tel: 977 241 514. Also Agencia Catalana de l'Aigua, Rambla Nova, 50, 43004 Tarragona. Tel: 977 214 556. Fax: 977 214 186.

Most waters are considered a relatively easy fish and retain a good reputation with the local angling community. Just a few minutes from your favourite beach destinations, a world of angling pleasure awaits you. Purchase a cheap fishing pole at the Décathlon de Tarragona, Torreolembarra district. Then buy your sweetcorn bait at the market.

Embalse Repsol, Riu Gaia, Tarragona and Salou, free fishing (carp, eels, and black bass). This is popular water. By the dam there are lots of smaller common carp and some royals. Bass go to 1kg by the rocks but are difficult to spot in other places. Use an earthworm jig, or black, brown and yellow spinners. Locate specimen carp by the bank, just below the surface. Most bait is successful here. Directions: just to the east end of Tarragona. From Molnars, on the N340, take the Catllar turn-off to Tarragona. The water is 200 metres behind the long beach.

Pantano de Fuix, near Sitges at Castelleta la Gornal, Riu Fuix, day ticket (carp, barbel, black bass and eels). Popular water with the Catalans, pole fishing is their speciality. It offers one of the best spots for carp in the area. But watch out for the trees behind you. Good for eels near the dam wall. For tickets: the petrol station between l'Arboc and Els Monjos, Benzinera Petrolan, N340, km1204, L'Arbos del P, tel: 977 670 551. It costs three euros. And at Esports Font C/Progres, 1 Vilafranca del Penedés, tel: 938 000 106. Directions: from Tarragona take the N340 east and exit at L'Arboc, right for Castelleta la Gornal. The lake is just south of town to your left. From Sitges go west C31 coast road, exit north at Vilanova i La Geltrú BV2115 for the Riu.

Pantà de Riu Decanyes, Cambrils, free fishing (carp and black bass). Clear water in a pretty spot. A lot of medium to large carp. Access from town is easy. Directions: from Cambrils take the T312/T313 to Riu Decanyes. Driving time: half an hour.

Castellón
de la Plana
Villarreal

Valencia

Sagunto   GOLFO DE VALENCIA

Valencia
Río Júcar   Torrent

Gandia

Dénia

Benidorm

Alicante

Valencia

CHAPTER THREE

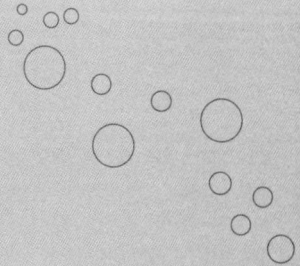

ince

egación Territorial de la Consejería de Agricultura
egori Gea, 27, 46009 Valencia. Tel: 963 866
nsejería de Medio Ambiente, Francisco Clavet, 7,
46011 Valencia. Tel: 963 869 853.

Angling Information: Federación Valenciana de Pesca, Pintor Ferrer
Calatayud, 7 Bajo, 46002 Valencia. Tel: 963 559 055, Fax: 963 559 280.
Email: olga@federacionpescacv.com

Boat licences: Confederación Hidrográfica del Júcar, Comisaría de
Aguas, Avda. Blasco Ibáñez 48, 46010 Valencia. Tel: 963 369 6350/393
8855. Fax: 963 938 801. Email: oficial@chj.mma.es or visit: www.chj.es

Directions are given for a start from Valencia unless otherwise stated.

Embalse de Arenos, Arenoso and Montanejos, free fishing (black bass,
carp, pike and barbel). Built in 1978. Small, clean mountain dam with
a colourful backdrop. The old town of Campos de Arenoso is now
submerged. High water level in winter. Low depth in summer can
make boat launching impossible. The bass are a bit small due to the
intermittent draining of the lake. Water is cloudy, which favours carp
fishing. Motor boats are allowed to within 250 metres of the dam wall.
Directions: northwest N234, exit Barracas, northeast 10km to Puentes
de Arenoso. Water is just southeast of here.

Embalse de Escalona, Navarres, Riu Cazunta and Riu Escalona, free
fishing (carp, black bass, pike, tench and eels). Built in 1992. Usually
a low water level. Strong fishing pressure and dam activity has had a
negative effect on the sport. Nonetheless, it remains a popular water.
Motorboats are prohibited within 250 metres of dam wall. Directions:
head south N430 exit at Alcudia de Crespins, go west C322 for 5 km
then north to Navarres. The water is nearby.

Marjal de Xeraco, Xeraco, free fishing (eels, black bass, perch and
llisa). A lake surrounded by orange orchards. The water is cloudy but
clean. Depth to 3 metres. Lots of wildlife. Directions: from Valencia go
south on the N332 towards Gandia. Xeraco (Jaraco) is on the left, just
past Tabernes de Valldigna.

Marjal de Pego, Oliva, Valencia-Alicante provinces, free fishing (black
bass and carp). A network of canals and rivers set in ricefields. Hard

fishing, but can be a very nice place to spend a few hours. Ancient laws prohibited women from fishing here for 500 years, but in 2001 two successfully petitioned the Junta to reclaim their rights. Good for bass up to 2.8kg, but bigger ones are harder to find. Fish for them in the north zone where the cross drains enter the lagoon, but not especially in the rivers Racon and Bullento. It's also good in the centre, at Riu de Baixos. This clear water lake is characterised by a lot of weed in the old narrow drainage channels. This makes spinning difficult, so go heavy. Try artificial poppers in summer to coincide with the elvers that arrive at this time. Vinyls and poppers in winter. Carp are abundant in the centre, and at the head of the Racon and Molinell rivers, by the game tanks. Barbel are still found in some holes and corners of the Bullento. Directions: south of Valencia on the coast road, N332, to Oliva, then take right towards Pego. Pego is 15 minutes inland from Denia.

> Ancient laws prohibited women from fishing at Marjal de Pego for 500 years, but in 2001 two successfully petitioned the Junta to reclaim their rights

Embalse de Contreras, Villargordo del Cabriel and Minglanilla, free fishing (carp, black bass, pike, barbel, and zander). Built in 1975. Good for bass all year round to 2kgs. Given the abundant woodland and bankside cover, the colour of your spinners is not critical. Live baiting with trout is allowed here. The perimeter of the lake is difficult to navigate because of the uneven terrain. The reservoir is never more than 50 per cent full, but the fish don't seem to mind. Motorboats not allowed within 3km of dam wall. They are only allowed between Villargordo del Cabriel and La Pesquera (Cuenca), towards the tail end of the water. Directions: from Valencia take the A3 west. After Utiel exit at Villargordo del Cabriel. The water is a few km to the northwest.

Río Turia, Gestalgar, free fishing (barbel, carp, trout, madrillas [bleak type]). Faster current alternating with deeper holes. A branch of the river has a small dam. A few trout, difficult to locate, but loads of barbel, mainly around Merendero zone. Directions: 49km west CV35. Turn off at Liria for Pedralba, Bugarra, and Gestalgar. Fish up the valley at Chulilla, *pesca sin muerte* (exit CV35 at Losa del Obispo) for trout. Locals use *lombriz cucharilla* (worm teaspoon) numbers 1 and 2 hook sizes.

Desembocadura del Carraixet, Alborea, free fishing (barbel, eels and mullet). A lot of mullet. Last part of channel is 25 metres wide and two metres deep. Directions: go west A3/E901 from Valencia to Requena. Drive southwest, N322, exit at Alborea. Go in the direction of the Alcampo Mercado (supermarket) towards the Els Peixets shrine.

Embalse Muela de Cortes, Cortes de Pallás, Río Júcar/Riu Xúquer, private, day tickets obtained in Cofrentes and Pallás (black bass, pike, bleak, eel, madrilla, pumpkinseed, zander and carp). This is one of the best bass waters in Spain. Many at three to five kilos. No-kill policy for bass from April 1 to May 31. No fishing on non-festive Mondays. Exploding bleak population, officially introduced in 1994, is main food source for bass. Magnificent scenery.

Limited bank access, boat is best. Trolling using an electric motor attached to the front of the boat is the way to go. A sonar device will soon locate any landmarks on the lake bottom that might harbour bass. A thermometer attached to a plumb line will decide their depth.

Live baiting is prohibited so bass and pike may only be caught on artificial baits. Use El Sher, Yensen and woodchopper lures. Blue and gold for spinner baits, green for vinyls. Pike average 5-8kg. Best in spring/summer: many caught on surface lures. Motor boats are allowed. Boat licence: (Confederación Hidrográfica in Valencia, see address above).

The steep-sided reservoir is set in a deep gorge in the Cortes hunting reserve, which shelters boar, wild goat and muflón. It runs 11km from the Compuertas (sluice gate) of the Embalse de Embarcaderos to the Presa de Muela de Cortes. Average depth: 30 to 65 metres. It's the only reservoir in the region that maintains a constant level.

There are three sections:

1. Forbidden zone, for boats and fishing, between the new dam-bridge of the Cortes de Pallás highway and the dam wall of Embalse de Cortes ll.
2. Free section between new dam-bridge of the highway of Cortes de Pallás and the Iberdrola security buoys. Only fishing from the bank here. Boats are allowed, but there are no launch sites in this area.
3. Private section from the buoys up to Embalse de Embarcaderos. Run by Club Valencia Bass and Bassmaster Alberic. Their email address is valenciabass@valenciabass.com. Fishing passes for the club section

can be purchased at Bar Niu D' Or in Alberic; Armeria Quinter, Sollana; Bar I Castro, Macastre; and Bar Fortunato and Bar Chema, Cortes de Pallás.

Directions: take the A3/E901 west from Valencia, exit at Requena. Go south, N330, exit at Cofrentes. Or take E901 and exit at Buñol, take CV425 south, tortuous route to Cortes de Pallás. One kilometre before Cortes de Pallás, turn right at crossing signposted "Bascula" and continue 2km to the water. Park a safe distance from the bank. Due to dam activity, the water level can change dramatically in just a few hours.

Embalse el Naranjero, Cortes de Pallás, free fishing (black bass, carp and bleak). Built in 1989. Clean water, pretty fauna. Banks can get steep. Water level can go up in a short time, so park away from the bank. Electric motors only. This will allow access to the remote spots. Directions: the only access is from Millares. Go from here to the dam.

Embalse de Forato, Macastre, free fishing (carp, barbel, bleak). Mostly carp, to one kilo. This is a good lake to use your plugs. The water is cloudy but clean. The depth is variable, in summer averages 2-3 metres. The beach banks are wide. Directions: from Valencia head west, E901/A3, exit at Buñol. Head south to Macastre, then west out to the water. You will have to cross over the dam wall then take a left for 1km. Mind the slope. Then take another left through the old campsite. Water is on other side. Park by the esplanade.

Embalse de Cofrentes, Cofrentes, free fishing (pike, black bass, carp and pumpkinseed). Zander have appeared here since 2000. Best swims in area for carp. Some barbel. Directions: go on the N430 towards Albacete. Exit 31 for Almansa then north past Ayora N330 to Cofrentes.

Embalse de Benagéber, Benagéber and Tuéjar, free fishing (black bass, pike, carp, barbel, eels and rainbow trout). Built in 1955. A mountain dam next to Reserva de Valdeserrillas. Unfairly neglected due to difficult topography and charisma of neighbouring waters. Obstinate, robust carp but a Mecca for Valencian big pike up to 16kg. Clear water, 10-12 metres deep, pretty surroundings full of red deer and muflón. The populous bass are best caught from a boat. All boat types permitted. The old town of Benagéber is submerged near the dam wall. Directions: from Valencia west, E901/A3. Exit at Utiel. North to Benagéber. Water is north of town, to left. Find tourist shelter, take a second left (unsurfaced road) to the water sports centre. There are two floating boat jetties here. The Adventuria water sports centre has canoes, sailboats, and a floating bar.

Asut de Antella, Antella, free fishing (pike, zander, carp, barbel and black bass). Small dam. A few big barbel. Directions: from Valencia head south on the N340 towards Alicante. Just after Alberic, before Xàtiva, turn west to Antella.

American largemouth black bass are the holy grail of Spanish freshwater fishing, with carp and barbel a poor second. The Iberian peninsula is an ideal environment. Bass have done best in waters flowing to the south and east, where the rivers and reservoirs sustain prolific bass populations.

Bass are considered great eating, as well as possessing fighting qualities second to none. Portuguese anglers allegedly sell the fish illegally for six euros a kilo to unscrupulous local restaurants across the border. Of course, Spanish anglers are never found guilty of such an offence.

Originally a native of the USA, largemouth bass were introduced to Spain by the Spanish Fisheries Office of the National Parks Department in 1955-56. The aim was to increase awareness of sport fishing in fresh water where summer temperatures rise above 20C but do not contain salmon. It was first introduced at the Aranjuez Hatchery near Madrid (minimum temperatures must fall below 16C at some time during the year if natural reproduction is to succeed). Three other hatcheries in Spain were established from 1965, at Plasencia del Monte (Huesca), El Palmar (Valencia) and Las Vegas de Guadiana Hatchery (Badajoz).

In Valencia and Andalusia annual bass growth rates are comparable with the best in the world. Individual fish frequently reach sexual maturity in less than 12 months. Large individual specimens are commonplace. The Spanish record is around four kilos. The world record stands at 10kg caught from Montgomery Lake in Georgia, USA.

Embalse El Regajo, Jérica, free fishing (carp, barbel and eels). Built in 1959. Motor boats allowed to within 250 metres of the dam wall. Its lovely tree-lined banks offer shade to anglers. Carp average 2-3kg. Best bait is sweetcorn, but most methods work. Three-star campsite with all usual amenities, or hostel accommodation. Directions: N234, 60km northwest, turn off at Segorbe towards Navajas. Water borders the town. Also go from Segorbe to the right on an unsurfaced road to the other end of the dam, next to the railway bridge that crosses the water.

Embalse de Sitjar, Onda, Ribesalbes, Río Mijares, free fishing (carp, barbel and eels). Built in 1960. Small water. Motor boats are allowed to within 250 metres of dam wall. There are few slipways but launching from the bank is fine. Stay at campsite. Directions: north N340 exit at Villarreal, west for Onda, C223 to Ribesalbes to the water.

Presa de Tous, Río Júcar/Riu Xúquer, Tous, free fishing (black bass, barbel, pike, pumpkinseed, bleak, carp, tench, eels and zander). On the afternoon of October 20,1982, the dam wall collapsed, with a balance of nine people dead and 27,000 made homeless. The new dam is 133 m a.s.l. and 1,300 metres long, the biggest in Spain when built. A big, deep water. Bass numbers used to be phenomenal, but have been cut back recently through (big) pike predation. Zander have entered through the *trasvase* (water transfer) between the Tajo and Segura rivers via the Río Júcar. Valencian anglers ignore the carp here. Difficult access and a long walk from the car to the shore. Motor boats are permitted. The only mooring point is a submerged bell tower of old Tous town, in middle of lake. Directions: south from Valencia on N340. Exit at Alberic and go west to Tous. Dam road is of restricted use, but good enough for your rental car.

> In 1982, the dam wall collapsed, killing nine people and leaving 27,000 homeless. The new dam is 133 metres high, one of the biggest in Spain

Río Júcar/Riu Xúquer, inland from Cullera (carp). River channel about 30 metres wide. Permanently pegged and used for a lot of Spanish matches. The water is controlled by the Spanish Angling Federation. There are carp to low double figures. The depth is five metres. The popular method to use is the quiver tip. The best bait is sweetcorn. Directions: follow N332 to Cullera. El Retorno, Río Júcar, Jalance, free fishing (carp, pike, and black bass, zander and bleak). Small, shallow lake with clear water. Rarely fished but worth a go. Directions: go west from Valencia on the E901/A3, exit at Requena. Go south on the N330. Jalance is south of Cofrentes.

Coto Fortaleny, Río Júcar, Fortaleny day ticket (carp). Three to seven metres deep. Good spot at the Fortaleny cemetery and by the ruins of Colomer tower. Directions: from Valencia head south on the E15 to Sueca. Fortaleny is just to the south.

Embalse de Buseo, Chera, free fishing (pike, barbel, black bass, carp, pumpkinseed). Bass have gone downhill. Water is infested with pumpkinseed (*perca sol*). A lot of barbel to 2kg where the river enters. Common and royal carp 3-5kg. Not so long ago there was an explosion of pike to 2kg but more recently they have landed bigger fish by the dam. A popular spot with English anglers is the muddy beach with easy acccess. Groundbait in the afternoon. Directions: from Valencia: west E901/A3, exit Requena for Chera. Exit here on to a track, due east to the water (about 5km).

> **→ Top Tip:** The reservoirs near Costa Blanca resorts go down during the tourist season. There are lots of small carp due to constant, ideal spawning conditions and no predation. This results in stunted fish growth. When water is low, cast to the middle and use a big hard boilie to deter the smaller fish and crayfish. For the big 'uns, travel inland to the big hydro-electric reservoirs, where mature fish populations exist due to natural predation. Here the aquatic vegetation is left relatively unhindered as a result of consistent water regulation.

Riba-roja de Túria, L'Eliana, day ticket (rainbow trout, barbel and madrillas). About 40 minutes from Valencia. Shallow, with some deep holes. Difficult access path. Home of El Suret fishing club. Pay by the bank. Directions: from Valencia go northwest to Lliria CV35, exit south to Villamarxant, then on to L'Eliana and Riba-roja.

Pantano de Loriguilla, Río Túria, Chulilla and Domeno (barbel and pike). Built in1967. Small, clean mountain dam in an attractive location. Water levels vary. At Domeno, a few km from Losa de Obispo, it's good for barbel and pike to 9kg. But there are no facilities for boats. Motor boats are allowed. This water will suit an inflatable craft, since at low water the banks can get steep. Directions: from Valencia take the CV35 beyond Lliria to Losa del Obispo. Access roads are a bit rough. Some only passable with a rented car. Where to stay? Sot de Chera has accommodation.

→ Top Tips for big-bass fishing in Spain

1. American largemouth black bass have excellent vision. When fishing relatively open or clear water, wear natural-coloured clothing. The bigger the bass, the older and cannier he will be, the easier he will get spooked.

2. Don't concentrate just on the retrieving action of the lure. Cast your lure in the correct place. The shady side of a log or rock, downstream side of stump or area of a fallen tree, and to weedbeds. If using a spinner, get it working immediately after entering the water, by jerking the rod. If using a worm or jig lure, cast in a lob that allows it to sink naturally, rather than in a sloping direction because of line pull. A popping type or surface lure cast with a lob will create the smallest disturbance on entry. The slower a surface popper lure is retrieved the better the chances of striking a bigger bass. Braided line offers the most control over the action of surface lures. Mono-filament has superior translucency, so is preferred for sinking lures. Here a lure going fast results in a more solid shot for the fish.

3. Fish are sensitive to vibration. Keep quiet. Avoid heavy footfalls on the bank. In a boat, avoid all unnecessary movement; use paddles to get the craft into position at a swim. An electric motor is used when trolling, sometimes at the front of the boat.

4. Bass are to be found at varying depths depending on temperature, light and food conditions. The ideal water temperature (this determines the correct oxygen level) for bass is 72-75 degrees. Water will stratify into different thermal layers, especially during the summer. Bass can always be located at a depth that matches their optimum water temperature. As the water heats up and down, the fish will naturally adjust their depth. Start with surface lures in the early morning then work your way deeper. Towards the evening reverse the pattern.

5. If you haven't got a boat, there are many lakes which offer daily hire by the shoreline. In addition, many of the waters listed in this guide will carry information about the local angling club, from which a vessel can usually be acquired.

6. Fish have a keen sense of smell. Wash your hands after handling boat fuel.

7. Every water feature has a fish lurking behind. It is just a matter of selecting the right lure with the right presentation to catch one.

↓ Alicante

It's easy to combine a holiday on the Costa Blanca with a few days fishing at the spots recommended here. All directions given are for a start at Alicante.

Angling licences: Delegación de Agricultura y Medio Ambiente, C/Churruca, 29, 03003 Alicante. Tel: 963 866 259/963 866 000. Expert advice has been kindly provided by Peter Gardiner, who runs angling holidays from his base near Benidorm (www.carp-fishing-spain.co.uk and petergardiner2001@yahoo.com). Ted Atkinson runs the local ex-pat Alcalalí angling club based on the Costa Blanca. Tel: 966 482 268. Angling matches are held bi-monthly at different venues. New members who have never fished before receive free expert tuition at this friendly club. An Alcalalí club match on the Río Júcar produced an average catch weight of 35kg,the winning weight being 90kg.

Embalse de Crevillente, Crevillente, free fishing (carp and barbel). Some: big specimens. Clear water, rocky bottom. It's ok to fish with heavy tackle. Use sweetcorn, maggots and floating crust. Directions: from Alicante take N340 southwest to Elche, continue to Crevillente. Dam is nearby.

Embalse de la Pedrera, Pantano de Torremendo, near Torrevieja, free fishing (carp, barbel and black bass). A pretty place for all the family. Underfished. Best spot is at the entrance to the water plant and at the opposite end to the dam underneath the Torreaguera crossing. The numerous submerged trees can be a hindrance. Take an umbrella, as there is no natural shade or water. Directions: southwest on A7, exit at Orihuela, go southeast via Hurchillo to Torremendo.

Embalse del Amadorio, Villajoyosa, free fishing (carp). Spot the carp on the surface from the raised bank. But take care as they are easily spooked. Fish to the north and west where there is good car access. Although shore paths here can be poor, it's only a short walk. On the opposite bank leave your car at the dam works. The environment is very barren, no trees. The water looks like a submerged quarry. Directions: A7 or N332 to Villajoyosa. Then northwest towards Orcheta.

Pantano de Beniarrés, Beniarrés, Río Serpis, free fishing (carp to 3kg and some eels). Dirty water recovering from pollution, but set in the mountains amid beautiful scenery. Few shady areas, but pleasant and quiet. Fish near dam or follow tracks down to waterside. Best fishing is from May to November. Pole can be deadly if the fish are close in. Directions: north N340 to Alcoy, continue to Muro de Alcoy then northeast to the town of Beniarrés. The road goes over the dam.

→ Recipe for grilled largemouth black bass (two servings)

3-4lb largemouth bass cut in 6oz fillets, skin removed
1 tablespoon butter
4 thin red onion slices
2 tablespoons sliced almonds
1 cup of sliced green onions
1/8 teaspoon salt
1/8 teaspoon paprika
1 sliced lemon

You will require medium heat for a grill or barbecue. On a greased aluminium foil sheet, roughly 50 by 40 cm, arrange two slices each of red onion and lemon over butter. Sprinkle over this one tablespoon of almonds and half of green onions. Then arrange fillets in a single layer over the onions, lemons and almonds. Top with remaining red and green onions, lemon and almonds. Season lightly with salt, pepper and paprika. Seal everything securely in foil. Put directly on grill for 11-15 minutes till fish begins to flake. Serve with a light salad, pasta, and plenty of vino. The perfect way to impress your non-angling friends and family with your newfound culinary skills. And it's a great way to round off a successful morning's fishing, Spanish style.

Embalse de Guadalest, Altea, near Benidorm, free fishing (carp, black bass, rainbow trout). The banks are quite steep in places but the long walk to the bank is worth it. Many carp that will take any bait. A lot of bass at the mouth of the Río Algar to 1.5kg, elsewhere they are fewer. Rainbow trout were introduced in 2000. Pines surround the lake and there is much wildlife. But watch out for the snakes! Directions: inland C3318 from Altea, at the town of Guadalest in the Sierra Serrella. Reservoir is to the north of town. Difficult access on right of water from Beniardá.

Murcia

CHAPTER FOUR

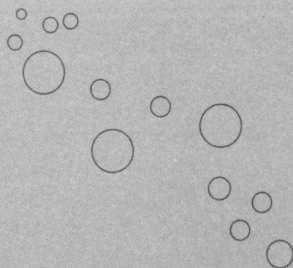

⬇ Murcia

Catch coarse fish in Murcia city centre. Although the bank may be too constricted for fishing with a pole, try using a telescopic rod.

Angling licences: Dirección General del Medio Ambiente, Oficina de Caza y Pesca, Catedrático Eugenio Ubeda Moreno, 3, 30071 Murcia. Tel: 968 362 628 & 968 283 918 & 968 228 913.

Further information: Federación Murciana de Pesca, C/Cánovas del Castillo, 29, 3a, 30003 Murcia. Tel/fax: 968 221 012   fprm@fprm.es

Boat licences: Confederación Hydrográfica del Segura, Comisaría de Aguas, Calle Plaza Fontes, 1, 30071 Murcia. Tel: 968 358 890/216 016. Fax: 968 211 845.

All directions given are for a start at Murcia.

Embalse de la Cierva, Mula, coto intensivo, day ticket (carp, black bass, barbel, rainbow trout). Reportedly, there is disabled access. Big carp to 23kg. Good for barbel. Nevertheless can be a hard fish. Boats allowed. Managed by the AMA (see above) and Mula fishing club. Directions: go west from Murcia past Alcantarilla (N 340), exit soon after onto C 415 west, for Mula. Water is just north of town.

Embalse Azud de Ojos, Río Segura, Archena, free fishing (carp, barbel and black bass). Good here for barbel and black bass. Shallow and does need dredging, but still 2-3 metres deep at the dam wall. Fish at the water wheel, 100 metres towards Ojos, and at the Embalse de Blaca, on the other side of the bridge. You can't drive this way. Leave the road on the Embalse de Blaca side near the dam in a place called Ca Mateo. Easy access to the water. Directions: Archena is northwest of Murcia off the A30.

Embalse de Argos, Calasparra, free fishing (barbel, carp and crucian). Top carp fishery in Murcia. Many carp to 3-5kg. Best in April and March. Still good in summer, but poor in winter. A hundred crucian in one morning. Good for barbel in autumn, groundbait with maggots by the dam and within a few feet of the bank. One problem is that the dam is always emptying. The water can be dirty and opaque, but has been cleaned up. Directions: from Murcia take the A30, exit left at Cieza. Head west for Cehegin C330 and C415. Turn right on to C3314 towards Calasparra. Before reaching the Cruce de Valentina, take a

PHOTO COURTESY OF BEACHCOMBER JOHN, MOJÁCAR ANGLING CLUB

Children too have a great time at the Embalse de Argos – pictured here is Rhys with a full net

right to the water. This is the first turn after the petrol station. Well-indicated and good access. Comment from John Wrenn, Mojácar Angling Club: Argos is one of our favourite waters in Murcia. It must have well over 100 swims but we have found the best by the dam wall. Deep water and, on average, bigger fish. Common and mirror carp and barbel too. There are definitely big fish in here as I have personally lost one, which took 30 metres of line off my reel in three separate runs. I have landed carp up to 27.5lb and fought with them up to 50lb and from my experience the Argos fish was 25lb or more.

> "There are definitely big fish in Argos as I have personally lost one, which took 30 metres of line off my reel in three separate runs..."

Embalse del Cenajo, Cenajo, free fishing (nase, red fish, barbel, carp, black bass and pike). Fish by the Cenajo dam wall. Live baiting for pike is allowed, a 13.5 kg pike was caught here on a Rapala recently. For bass use *lombriz* (worm) lures, spinners, and vinyls. Directions: Murcia A30 northwest, exit at Hellín and southwest to Cenanjero, C3212. Cenajo reservoir via CM412. Or go via the Embalse de Camarillas.

Embalse de Camarillas, Las Minas and Calasparra, free fishing (barbel, black bass, and carp). Nearly as clean as Cenajo but the water level varies greatly in summer. Use sweetcorn, maggots and boilies. The banks slope quite steeply in places. Good here for barbel. It has better access than at Cenajo. Directions: Murcia A30 northwest, exit west for Calasparra C3314. Then north for La Esperanza. Take the road that goes to Cenajo. Go past the turn-off for Canejo for 5km to Las Minas, past the cemetery, then turn left behind the village to the dam.

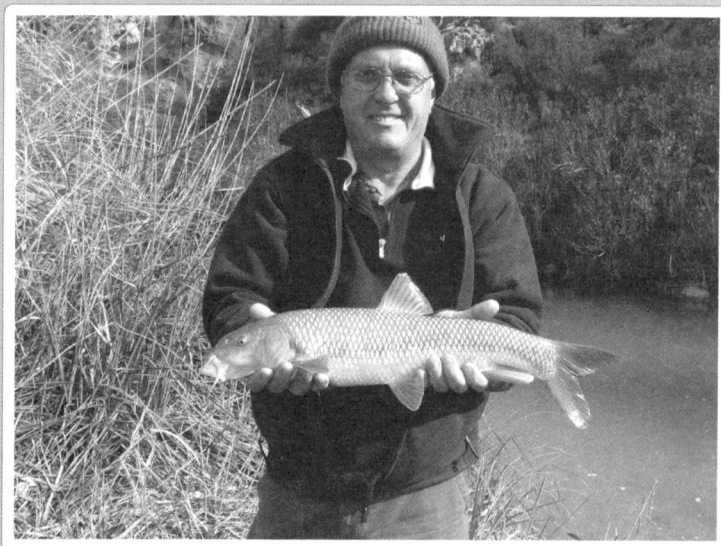

PHOTO COURTESY OF BEACHCOMBER JOHN, MOJÁCAR ANGLING CLUB

John Wrenn with a 3.75lb barbel caught on the Río Segura near the Cenajo hotel in the Murcia region — there are nice trout here too

Ayamonte

Huelva

Córdoba

Linares

Jaén

Río Guadalquivir

Sevilla

Río Genil

Granada

Antequera

Jerez de la Frontera

Almería

*GOLFO
DE CÁDIZ*

Cádiz

Málaga

CABO DE GATA

Marbella

Gibraltar (UK)

MEDITERRANEAN SEA

ESTRECHO DE GIBRALTAR

Andalusia

CHAPTER FIVE

↓ Andalusia

So you've made it to Andalusia. Heard great things about the fishing, but want to know where the action is. Listed below are scores of wonderful angling destinations, many just a stone's throw from the popular Costa holiday resorts. Go a little further inland and experience near-virgin waters and magnificent scenery.

Be warned: it gets extremely hot inland in July and August, 30 to 40 degrees C. However, the hotel prices are the coolest in Spain. The countryside is greener than most expect and the environment is as clean as it is beautiful.

The industrial revolution gave the south of Spain a miss so its lakes and rivers have been left largely untouched by pollution and modern development, except for dam- building, the national sport. Sadly, the Atlantic sturgeon now rarely visits the Río Guadalquivir.

As Andalusia covers a large area, the guide divides it into eight sections, the provinces of Almería, Granada, Málaga, Cádiz, Huelva, Seville, Córdoba and Jaén. Where to start? A water in one province may have its immediate neighbour in another, e.g. the Zufre reservoir in Huelva province is only a few kilometres from that of Cala in adjacent Seville. Keep your plans flexible, so that if one location for fishing is unsuitable the next destination will only be a short journey time away.

What makes Andalusia popular today with anglers is its great fishing and a shared respect for the wonderful outdoors.

Information about all aspects of Andalusia, including tourism, can be found at: www.andalucia.org; www.andalucia.com; and www.juntadeandalucia.es

For information on reservoir water levels in the region visit www.agenciaandaluzadelagua.com/v2/pantanos.php

---

Licences

All fishermen are required to carry a licence issued by Andalusia's environmental department, the Consejería de Medio Ambiente. Go to any Agencia de Medio Ambiente (AMA) office — addresses are given for each province — or any branch of these banks: Unicaja, CajaMar, Caja Rural de Granada, Caja Rural de Córdoba, Caja Rural de Jaén, Caja

---

Rural del Sur (Sevilla y Huelva), Banco de Andalucía (tel: 902 301 000), Banco Popular Español (tel: 902 301 000). You can also obtain a licence via the AMA website (see below). Licences are available for 15 days, one, three or five years. They are free for under-16s and over-65s. A two-rod licence is issued for coarse fishing only. For trout fishing you pay a small supplement.

Proof of identity and previous experience are required. Take copies of your passport (if resident in Spain, bring two copies of a "letter of residence" from your local town hall) and an angling licence from any country or Spanish region issued between January 5, 1991, and January 5, 1996. Unofficially, any current or old angling licence will do, in lieu of taking an official, three-day angling course. In the late 1990s Andalusia's Medio Ambiente decided to set up a computer system dealing with all licence applications for the region. However, this system is unable to distinguish between licence applications for hunting and angling. This is why angling licence applicants may be subjected to an unnecessary exam, in the same way that hunting licence applicants are (for health and safety).

If you are really unlucky, you may be asked to present, in addition to the above, an officially translated copy of your British angling licence. This must be authenticated, by a solicitor for instance. Also, residents may need to show a copy of their NIE document (NIE is the identification number for tax purposes).

The licence fee is €39.85, which is valid for five years and covers fishing for trout. Shorter periods and coarse angling licences are available for as little as €12.

Public liability insurance for anglers is mandatory and must be obtained when seeking a licence. If you have Spanish household insurance, the policy number will cover this procedure.
If you have a problem, call freephone 900 850 500, or email: cazaypesca.cma@juntadeandalucia.es. www. juntadeandalucia.es. This site gives all the information concerning licences for the region. Over-65s can arrange a free licence on-line.

Note: The Mojácar Angling Club can sort out an angling licence on your behalf – see next section on Almería.

A booklet called *Manual of the Fisherman* is published by Mailing Andalusia. To obtain a copy, call 954 237 040 or 954 236 863.

⬇ Almería

Almería province is one of the sunniest and driest corners of Spain, where scores of spaghetti Westerns have been filmed. The desert terrain limits fishing opportunities, but you can still find good spots to cast your line.

Licences for freshwater coarse fishing: Delegación Provincial de Medio Ambiente, Centro Olivares, Bloq. Singular, 2a Planta, 04071 Almería. Tel: 950 012 800.

Embalse del Almanzora, Cuevas del Almanzora, free fishing (carp and barbel). Directions: north from Almería N340, N344, exit east for Cuevas del Almanzora. The lake is just to the north of town. Mojácar Angling Club reports it's hard to find a fishable swim. At the lock gates end there are too many snags and access to most of the lake is difficult due to steep cliffs. More information: Federación Andaluza de Pesca, León Felipe, 2-bajo, 04007 Almería. Tel/fax: 950 151 746. Email: federacion@fapd.org. www.fapd.org

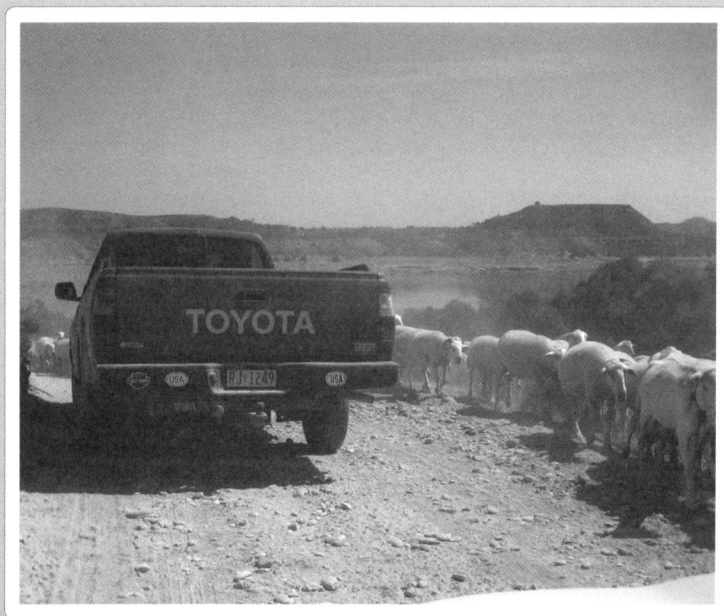

PHOTO COURTESY OF BEACHCOMBER JOHN, MOJÁCAR ANGLING CLUB

As this picture shows, it's not always easy to get to your swim!

Mojácar Angling Club (MAC) was founded in 2005 by expats living in Almería. Member John Wrenn reports on angling opportunities in his area.

We coarse fish every Wednesday either in Andalusia or the Murcia region. On Sundays we fish from the beach or rocks in or around Mojácar and on one or two days a week we boat-fish out of Garrucha.

The Embalse del Negratín, just outside the town of Zújar in Granada province and a two-hour drive from Mojácar, is the biggest one around. The best swims by far are the ones close to the spa baths but there are only about eight. There are a couple of fishable swims at the end of the concrete boat access ramp, literally underneath the restaurant. Diners sometimes throw bread into the lake from the restaurant and big fish are often seen hanging around.

> "A 100lb bag in five hours is not uncommon for one of our pole-fishing members..."

There are much better swims on the other side of the lake, found by driving through the village of Cuevas del Campo at the end of a 9km dead-end road. It takes around 20 to 30 minutes' extra driving time from Mojácar. The swims here are less snaggy, but fish are not waiting to be fed as at the spa baths. We have caught mirror and common carp, barbel, brown and rainbow trout. There are black bass and chub. Fishing for carp is mostly with sweetcorn and quite heavy regular groundbaiting is required to keep fish feeding. A 100lb bag in five hours is not uncommon for one of our pole-fishing members. Most fish caught tend to be 3/4lb to 1.5lb with 3 to 4lb fish being the biggest of the day. I use10lb mainline with 6lb hook length until the fish get into a feeding frenzy then go straight through with the heavier line. Even though these fish are hungry the bigger ones have learned not to get caught. We have been broken by big fish which, believe me, fight like they have never been caught before. Even a 1.5lb fish can feel like a double for the first few seconds.

Another reservoir in Granada province is the Embalse de Francisco Abellán sometimes known as La Peza Lake (just off the A92 near Guadix). In late 2005, after prolonged drought, only at the far end of →

→ the track could you find deep water with bigger fish. Also there are a couple of swims down from the restaurant at the dam wall. The biggest I caught there is 4.5lb common carp on my first and only visit.

Just inside the Murcia region is Embalse de Puentes, a 20-minute drive from the town of Lorca. Deep water can be reached easily but there are only about eight swims. At a swim by the lock gates – you need to climb down – I've seen very big fish on the surface there. There were both types of carp and one that could be an F1 hybrid type. They have a lateral line like a barbel so could be barbel/common carp crosses. Black bass and trout are around too and plenty of turtles. From the end of October onwards, as the sun does not rise high enough to shine on most of the swims, it's cold.

John Wrenn offers to sort out your angling licence for Andalusia or Murcia for a small charge. His address: The Beachcomber Bar/Restaurant, Box 33, Avda Andalucía, 22 edif Multicentro, local 25, 04638 Mojácar, (Almería). Tel. 950 473 099.
Email: beachcomberjohn@gmail.com

↓ Granada

Fed by the snows of the Sierra Nevada, which towers over the city of Granada, once the capital of a Moorish kingdom, the waters of this province offer some worthy challenges.

Purchase licences at: Delegación Provincial de Medio Ambiente, C/ Marqués de la Ensenada, 1, 18071 Granada. Tel: 958 026 000. Fax: 958 026 058. Email: delegado.gr.cma@juntadeandalucia.es

Additional information: Francisco Hurtado Moles, Federación Andaluza de Pesca Deportiva de Granada, Hera del Cura, 20, 17170 Alfacar (Granada). Tel: 670 970 401.

Riofrío (trout). Visit this popular spot to fish — and eat — trout. There are many restaurants here serving excellent trout dishes. The Frío and Salado rivers offer super trout fishing up to 5kg. Average catch is seven to nine fish per day. The season is all year. The fish limit is 10. Directions: follow the A92 from Granada to Málaga. Riofrío is west of Loja in the

Sierra de Loja. Trout licences (Licencia de Pesca Fluvia) available from: Albergue de Pescadores de Riofrío, Riviera de Riofrío s/n, 18300 Loja (Granada). Tel: 958 323 177.

Embalse de los Bermejales (carp, gypsy barbel, Iberian nases, and black bass). Twelve barbel possible in a short afternoon session, average weight 1.5kg. Try method feeder on sweetcorn or PVA bags using boilies. Some immense carp lurk here. A popular competition venue. Pretty location. It offers easy access, as there is a perimeter road on which you can drive right around the lake to locate a suitable swim, 45 minutes by car. The entrance is by the *presa* (dam wall). Try by the water plant although this can be left high and dry in dry years, like 2005. A good swim is on the spur just down from the northeast side of the reservoir where you can drive almost directly to the water's edge. Directions: from Granada, take highway south towards Motril on the coast, soon branching west on the A338 southwest through Armilla towards Alhama de Granada. The spectacularly situated town of Alhama has hot springs (take the plunge at the Hotel Balneario, 2km east).

Embalse de Cubillas (carp, pike and barbel). Recommended barbel water. Fish at the Calicasas bank. Buy your day ticket in the village of Chaparral, at the Bar San Isidro (excellent tapas), next to the church and town hall. There are just a few pike but they grow large. Small bass exist in only a few places and are difficult to catch. A lot of small carp to one kilo. For bigger carp use floated baits or large hard baits for the bottom. This is a pretty lake with good access. It gets busy at weekends. Hence there is a litter problem. On Sundays swimmers and jet-skis take over. Directions: head north from Granada on the N323, after 15km exit right for Diefontes/El Chaparral. Head for Restaurante Romero. Turn right at dam wall for La Torre. Before the entrance to the Zona Recreativa, but after the clay pigeon centre (Tiro de Pichón), head for La Cencela (road junction). It has an iron gate. The best access is on the far shore along the old main road (N321) that goes around the water, past the obsolete Calicasas railway station. There is a campsite bankside by the old road.

Embalse de Béznar, Pinos del Valle, day ticket (carp, mullet and black bass). For tickets, tel: 958 276 550. Carp up to five kilos, averaging one to two kilos, 100 in a day. And a few big ones. Try the left bank heading downstream. Use large boilies to deter the abundent smaller carp. Smaller number of good bass to 3.5kg. Very pretty spot, but best in spring. Access for car can prove problematic. Directions: One hour from Nerja, along N340 then north from Motril up the N323 towards

Granada. Exit at Béznar. Head west on minor road towards Pinos del Valle. The road will take you over the dam wall. Turn right at Pinos for Restábal, which is at the tail-end of the water. Fish from here on the Río Ízbor on the stretch leading to the embalse. Catch medium-sized carp on sweetcorn using method feeder or simple ledger rig.

Embalse de Francisco Abellán, La Peza, Lopera, free with special regulations (carp, black bass, barbel, trout). Pretty lake surrounded by mountains but few access points. A lot of small carp up to 7kg, few black bass, barbel and trout (must be returned) in Río Fardes. Good fishing near La Peza, good food nearby at café La Fuente La Gitana. Good-size barbel in lake by the town. Good, easy fishing for carp and barbel by the dam at Lopera. Directions: from Granada take A92 east towards Guadix, exit at Lopera. For La Peza take old road off A92, access is from Dario crossing. Access also from dam area by restaurant at Lopera. (See also comment by John Wrenn in Almería section.)

Embalse de Canales, Río Genil, Güéjar Sierra, free with special regulations (carp). Baits permitted in trout season (high mountain regulations) are boilies and spinners. Otherwise sweetcorn and broad bean. Five trout limit. Directions: half hour east of Granada along Genil valley to Güéjar Sierra.

Embalse de Colomera, carp fishery, tel: 958 276 550 (tench, carp and barbel). Barbel are few in number and streetwise. Smaller number of carp than at Béznar, but bigger and better fighters. Mirror carp to five kilos. Fewer commons. This is a good place for pole fishing as many fish are caught at the margins on sweetcorn, but they may move further out towards noon. Groundbait regularly to keep them interested. The banks can get muddy. Fish the left bank heading downstream. A calm and relaxing family spot. Directions: from Granada head north on the N323, exit left for GR220 to Colomera. Take the narrow road north out of Colomera. Carry on right at the fork for Benalúa de las Villas, the water will be on your left. Take a left for the dam wall, shortly after the fork for Benalúa.

Embalse del Negratín, Zújar, free fishing (carp and barbel). A big water but easy to circumnavigate. Fish the left bank heading downstream. Bass although small are voracious. This is a good barbel location. Carp to a lesser extent. There is a lot of weed during summer, when it can get noisy at weekends. Your fish will get lost on the snaggy bottom, so use a break leader for your cheap weights. Look out for Granada's own Ayers Rock, on your way north out of Zújar. Pozo Alcón, a tourist centre, has Camping Municipal La Bolera, many hotels and casas rurales. Directions: from Granada head east on the A92. At Baza, head north on the C323 to Zújar. Turn left here for the dam wall on the A315. It will be on your right just off this road, after the Freila turn off, but before Cuevas de Campo. Alternatively, if you continue past Zújar on the C323, the road reaches the eastern part of the reservoir.

⬇ Málaga

You can easily combine a beach holiday at one of the Costa del Sol resorts with a few days' angling. Reservoirs and rivers are within easy reach of the coast. Purchase your licence at: Delegación Provincial de Medio Ambiente: c/ Mauricio Moro Pareto, Edf. Eurocom, Bloq. Sur, Plantas 3 y 4, 29071 Málaga. Tel: 951 04 00 58. Fax: 951 04 01 08. Email: delegado.ma.cma@juntadeandalucia.es

Information: Manuel Hijano Reina, Federación Andaluza de Pesca Deportiva Málaga, Carrera, 23-4, 29200 Antequera (Málaga). Tel: 952 843 915. Mobile: 670 970 404. Email: manu553@eresmas.com

Boat licences: Confederación Hidrográfica del Sur, Comisaría de Aguas, Paseo Reding, 20, 29016 Málaga. Tel: 952 126 700. Fax: 952 211 546. www.chse.es. This water board covers Algeciras, Marbella, Málaga, Vélez-Málaga, Motril, and Almería.

Oficina Municipal de Turismo, Avda de Cervantes, 1, Paseo del Parque, Málaga. Tel: 952 134 730. www.malagaturismo.com

"Andalusia is unique", according to the Málaga Tourist Office. They are right. One Spanish angler, irate at the decimation of his favourite black bass lake by the ubiquitous *perca sol*, decided that the solution was to introduce its natural predator: another American visitor, the *piranha*.

Problem solved? A local paper reported that "a mystery fish" had bitten a swimmer. Rumours that *piranhas* had been found in an Andalusian water raising the horrendous possibility that they might breed were borne out when a spearfishing club investigated. They speared and killed two of the little horrors in the Embalse de Guadelteba (Málaga). How many more are lurking in this vast stretch of water? ➔

→

There have been several further reports of these fish being taken from widely separated waters, including the Río Turia in Valencia. One was taken from the Río Las Cañas near Gibraltar. It weighed over one kilo.

Embalse de la Concepción, Marbella, free fishing (barbel and carp). Steep banks make access difficult. Try by Istán country club, which has fishing boats for hire and a fishing committee headed by Richard Hewitt. Directions: 7km from Marbella on N340, then head north towards Istán. Water is to the left of the road before you reach Istán.

Embalse de la Viñuela, Torre del Mar, carp fishery (carp and gypsy barbel). Has recently been restocked with bass. Day tickets no longer available on site, but they are still officially required from the Medio Ambiente in Málaga (one euro a day). Mostly the regular Guardia Civil patrols require only presentation of the regional licence.

This water is widely regarded as a consistent fish. Best to start at the

PHOTO COURTESY OF BEACHCOMBER JOHN, MOJÁCAR ANGLING CLUB

Embalse de la Viñuela: Big Steve stalked a black bass with a piece of preserved sardine

recreational area near the dam wall. Space here for 100 anglers, in particular by the corner of the dam nearest the extraction tower but fishing right next to the dam is not permitted. Sweetcorn works well on a hair rig using method feeder. But maize is better still, being that much more durable. For ground bait locals purchase packets of pre-roasted bread purchased for two euros from *supermercados*. Punched English-style bread purchased frozen is preferred for hook bait, using slider float or swimfeeder.

The mornings are poor. Groundbait at this time, then go and have a good lunch. Schools of carp patrol the fringes at dusk (the best time), especially by the *pesquil* (fishery) and by the landing stage near the Hotel La Viñuela (tel: 952 519 193), which has good views over the lake. By the west bank is Camping Presa La Viñuela, tel: 952 030127. Directions: from Málaga head east on the N340. Exit at Torre del Mar, go north on the A335, veer right towards Alhama. Turn left soon after for Cortijuelos and lakeside.

Embalse del Limonero, Málaga, free fishing (carp and barbel). Catches are not as abundant as before the 1995 drought. This doesn't mean they're poor, just no longer superb. There is an excessive small carp population. Bass up to one kilo are easily caught. Floating crust is recommended bait for the re-emerging bigger carp. Water levels fluctuate a lot. Try for bass at the Río Guadalmedina below the dam. Limonero is officially a trout water, although no one has seen one there recently. Directions: just to the north of Málaga city, west of the N331.

Embalse del Guadalteba-Guadalhorce, Antequera and Campillos. This lake system is located north of El Chorro, a mighty gorge and south of Campillos. The water is divided into three huge reservoirs: 1. Embalse del Conde del Guadalhorce to the south. 2. Embalse del Guadahara to the east. 3. Embalse del Guadalteba to the west. These recovered from the early 1990s drought but levels were low again in 2005. Note that temperatures rise above 35C from May to October. There is little shade around the lakes when the water has receded. A cooling wind can be deceptive. Suncream, hats and a brolly are essential.

Embalse del Conde del Guadalhorce, free fishing, mostly mirror carp averaging 1.5-2kg and barbel. A 7kg pike was caught in 1999. Best in spring and autumn. Not very deep, even lower in summer. Shoreline is gravel or rocks. Directions: head for Ardales from Campillos, C342, follow signs for water. The dam is 2 km up from Ardales. Easy access to water. Locals fish in the swimming section to the left of the dam. From

PHOTO COURTESY OF TERRY JORDAN

The scenic Guadalhorce lakes

Málaga (60 km away), go north on A357, exit at Pizarra for El Chorro, via Álora, then west on MA444 past Bobastro. Turn off at 3km, go for 2.5km to a T-junction. Turn left to the south down a dirt track 1.5km to the peninsula. Best spot is just out from the cove on the right 1km to the south of the T-junction via the dirt track.

Guadalteba, free fishing (carp, black bass, barbel). Fish at Peñarrubia for carp (to 10kg, 2000). But there are lots of terrapins here. At water's edge it is two metres deep, in the middle much deeper. No boats are allowed, but it can get busy as the beautiful scenery attracts many campers and swimmers. These are not considered a problem by anglers. The fishing is good in the clear water by the dam wall, even if sometimes a little windy. The shoreline is sand and gravel beaches. Autumn and winter are good for big barbel and big carp. In April the water is transparent and easy to fish. In summer there are a lot of small carp. Use big boilies to negate the problem. Beans and potatos are also good local baits. Fish of 5-6kg are hard to catch here. Since the drought of 1995, barbel, pike and black bass have not recovered to previous levels or size. But some spots are paved with small carp. Black bass are a popular catch. Directions: From Málaga, go north, A357, come off at Pizarra for El Chorro. From Antequera, A382 west to Campillos, then south on A357 to Peñarrubia. Best spot is to the left of the dam down a dirt track.

Embalse del Guadahara, free fishing (carp, barbel, black bass). This lake is a personal favourite of British angler Terry Jordan who reports: "The fish fight extremely hard and feel twice the size by its rocky shoreline. The best spot I found was to the left down a slip road by the restaurant 2km from the Campillos dam crossing towards Antequera. After roughly 0.5km take a left down a dirt track to the shoreline. Here you should cast 30m into the channel. The banks are muddy with rocks. For a six-hour session I recommend taking 1kg boilies (15mm) or pellets and 30 PVA mesh bags. For my last trip I stayed at Álora in the friendly, British-run El Azul Guest House (www.elazulspain.com), about a 20-minute drive from the lakes. Below Álora the Río Guadalhorce holds barbel to 2kg, best fished early evening under the iron bridge."

Parque Ardales (camping and apartments, tel: 952 112 401) is 7km north of Ardales by the reservoir, canoes and bikes for hire. Other possibilities: La Posada del Conde, comfortable hotel with good restaurant, Pantano del Chorro, tel: 952 112 411; Apartamentos la Garganta, near El Chorro station, tel: 952 495 298, fax: 952 495 298; Camping El Chorro, tel: 952 112 696. El Chorro, east of Ardales and north of Álora, is the centre for mountaineering in Andalusia. Here the Río Guadalhorce flows through the Garganta del Chorro, an impressive gorge hundreds of metres deep.

Fishing the Guadalhorce

Veteran angler Norman Smith has spent half his life living and fishing in Spain. His articles, particularly on carp fishing, have appeared in numerous specialised publications. Contact Norman if you have any questions on angling in Andalusia at normansmith@terra.es Here he reports on his backyard, the Río Guadalhorce, which reaches the sea just west of Málaga.

"The Río Guadalhorce is the small winding channel that you can clearly see as you fasten your seat belt to descend at Málaga airport. It rises as a glorified ditch around Antequera, feeding into El Chorro and exiting through a steep gorge, levelling out below the mountain village of Álora. Fishing is prohibited on sections leading in and out of the reservoirs (to the north of El Chorro). The river rarely exceeds 30 metres in width and hardly ever a metre in depth. Light tackle is best, free line with a single swan-shot ledger. For bait, buy local sweetcorn, luncheon meat, small cubes of potato or floating crust.
→

→ The fishing really starts on my doorstep at Villafranco del Guadalhorce, below the confluence with the Río Grande. From Málaga take the A357 road west, past Campanillas. At this point the valley is exceptionally beautiful and is home to herons, grebes, mallards, cormorants and birds of prey. Turn down the side of the Río Grande petrol station, past the Cártama aerodrome, home to fire-fighting planes in summer, to a dirt road that runs along the river. After the first autumn rains the fish move up into this area.

Downstream, access is easier on the opposite bank close to Aljaima. Reach it via the C337 Málaga-Álora road. Near to the signposted Cártama Crocodile Park, traverse the level crossing to the river. (Some "crocs" have escaped into the river. Fully grown, they can weigh up to 580 kilos, rather more than the average fighting bull. When I heard the park was being relocated to Torremolinos, I thought the problem had moved away from my doorstep. Then a Nile crocodile was captured by a Guardia Civil patrol at a ford in the Pizarra area!)

River access is also possible at the Estación de Cártama. Park underneath the road bridge which crosses the channel. From this point, the river holds a second species of barbel that reaches double figures. Big eels are a plus. My son Stuart has landed a 5lb barbel just downstream. This is a popular spot so avoid holiday times.
Look out for huge shoals of elusive grey mullet at Cortijo Mestanza weir, where they reach double figures. Sadly, the fishing hasn't recovered from dredging here in 1999.

About four kilometres from Churriana on the MA417, which leads to Cártama, turn on a roundabout towards Barriadas Peñon and Zapata. Continue on a narrow road past large residential developments and ask for the best access to the river. The river can also be approached from the main coastal highway, the N340. Turn off into the industrial estate (*poligono industrial*), which lies just east of the airport, and look for small access roads upstream of the sewage works (*depuradora*). This tidal stretch holds huge shoals of mullet, carp and barbel."

Río Fuengirola, Fuengirola, free fishing (carp, barbel, Iberian nases and eels). Small, pretty river. Fish by the Castillo de Sohail. Directions: the water stretches 2km from the sea at Fuengirola.

Río Grande, Coín, free fishing (barbel and eel). Half-hour drive from

Málaga, Marbella and Torremolinos. Despite its name this isn't a big river. It dries up in the summer months but gets repopulated in winter by fish from the Río Guadalhorce. Catch barbel here between 1.5 to 2lb. Otherwise, a good quality location surrounded by woodlands. Clear water can be a problem, as are the terrapins. A good spot for barbel is often by the San Augusto electric power station. Catch them on a golden nymph fly, up to 5kg. You don't need a fly rod. Use a bubble with one or two droppers tied with suitable flies off your main line. Culinary freshwater clams are this river's speciality. Directions: west from Málaga on A357, then A355 towards Coín, then accessible via country roads. The river fishes well between Coín and Alozaina.

Embalse Las Medranas, San Pedro de Alcántara, near Marbella, free fishing (carp). A mostly clean water with tidy banks. Carp 2 to 5kg. Water depth is from 1.5 to 5 metres in the middle. Directions: west from Marbella along the N340 to San Pedro. Take the Ctra de Ronda which runs around town to the north, then left at a roundabout with a petrol station and past the Recinto Ferial on Avenida Las Medranas.

Río Genal, near Casares. Catch mountain barbel (Andalusian) on ledgered sweetcorn in the fast current. Use 2oz weights. Directions: From Estepona take N340, then inland on MA546 to Casares. River is west of Casares. Locate wind turbines and follow track from village to the channel.

⬇ Cádiz

A rewarding angling experience. Access to some waters may require crossing agricultural pasture. For the relatively fit, hardly a problem. Nonetheless, it's worth bearing in mind that the Cádiz region is famous for breeding fighting bulls. Usually their presence is advertised by boards bearing the words "*Ganado bravo*". For this reason only anglers of the very highest fitness level should share a field with even the smallest hint of bovine activity.

Licences: Delegación Provincial de Medio Ambiente, Pl. Asdrúbal, s/n-3 (esquina Amilcar Barca), 11071 Cádiz. Tel: 956 008 700. Fax: 956 008 702/956 008 703. Email: delegada.ca.cma@juntadeandalucia.es

Information: José Luis Ganfornia Márquez, Federación Andaluza de Pesca Deportiva Cádiz, Taura, 24, 11406 Jerez de la Frontera (Cádiz). Tel/fax: 956 335 927, mob 696 767 869. Email: cádiz@fapd.org

Embalse de Zahara de la Sierra, El Gastor, free fishing (carp, nase, barbel, and black bass). This is a deep-water dam where you can smell the mountain air. Oxygen-rich water continually feeds this pretty lake in the middle of the Ronda sierras.

The fishing is good at Esparradosilla. Another good place is by the old mill brook (*arroyomolino*). The opposite bank is its equal. It has a recreational area with good access and parking, by the Gastor road. The third place is by the dam wall. Here there is also good parking, and a recreation zone. A good spot for bass and some big carp. The water is used by the Guadalcobacín de Arriate fishing club and has hosted the Spanish National Federation championships.

Directions: from Ronda go northwest, C339 to Zahara. From Jerez, east on A382 past Arcos and Villamartín, exit at Algodonales, south C339, the water is just before Zahara, dramatically situated with an eighth-century Moorish castle. Take the local road that passes over the dam wall. Then choose your path to the bank.

Where to stay? Hostal Marqués de Zahara, Tel: 956 123 061, 956 137 261, Calle San Jaume 3. Camping Arroyomolinos, Tel: 956 234 079, near the reservoir. Grazalema Park information, Tel: 956 12 3 114.

Sierra de Grazalema Natural Park is famous for its trout fishing and hill walking (spring and autumn are best). Europe's southernmost trout stream is at El Bosque. Free permits are required. They can be booked in advance and , if preferred, collected at Zahara. Contact the Oficina del Parque Natural de la Sierra de Grazalema, Avda. Diputación s/n, 1160 El Bosque (Cádiz). Tel: 956 716 063/716 236.
Email: Ecoturismo@egmasa.es

Embalse de los Hurones, Algar, free fishing (carp and barbel). Directions: From Jerez take A382 to Arcos, then southeast on CA5221 to Algar. Continue past Algar then look for small road on the left, heading north to El Charco de los Hurones. The dam is nearby.

Embalse de Arcos, Arcos, free fishing, (carp, nase, barbel and black bass). The water is clear, 3-4 metres deep. There are facilities here. Baits to use include sweetcorn. Big bags of carp: 30kg in five hours. Too hot in June. The lake lies below the medieval town of Arcos perched high on a cliff. Accommodation at the cheap but very clean hostal/bar Mesón de la Molinera, restaurant and terrace overlooking the lake. You can fish from here. Their chalets are two metres from the water's edge, therefore not suitable for small children. Also by the water is Camping Lago de Arcos, Tel: 956 708 333/700 514. Arcos Tourist Office, Plaza del Cabildo, Tel: 956 702 264. Directions: from Jerez northeast A382, 30km to Arcos. Go northeast of town.

Embalse de Guadalcacín, Arcos, by the dam wall, free fishing (carp, pike, barbel and black bass). Magnificent scenery. Clear water that goes deep (3-5 metres at the edge). This water holds the best bass population in Spain. It holds the national record, at 4kg and 40cms. Its secret is that not many fish here. Moving along the bank can get difficult since much of the perimeter land is private.

Only the dam zone has easy access, but it is still a good fish despite heavy pressure. Pike to 21.45kg was caught in 1989. Impressive carp to13kg, and barbel to one metre in length, by the bank. The tail end is more complicated to fish. Here the big barbel will go after the bass spinners from the boat. Motor engines are not allowed. Careful, as snorkel divers hunt with harpoons here at the weekends, even though it is illegal.

Embalse de Guadalcacín II, Arcos, free fishing (carp, nase, barbel and black bass). Clear water year round, can get windy, stony ground. It's easy to catch carp here to one kilo. A lucky chap had six bass to 13kg recently. Fish for them under sunken trees at the fringes, where the bank is bordered with pines. The ground is earthy which makes the bottom muddy. Find the big barbel by the dam. They grow up to one metre long. The Andalusian fishing championships have been held here, so there is lots of room. The reservoir is surrounded by magnificent scenery. The nearby town of Algar has a campsite. Directions: from Jerez take the A382 east, exit at Arcos. From here go to San José de Valle, 10km southeast, CA52, to the water.

> It's easy to catch carp here to one kilo. A lucky chap had six bass to 13kg recently. Fish for them under sunken trees at the fringes, where the bank is bordered with pines.

Río Guadiaro, by the mouth (*desembocadura*), free fishing (barbel, roach). Barbel average two kilos, up to five kilos, lovely setting. Recommended tactics include freelined snail found underneath bamboo shoots bankside. Earthworm is a killer. Water extraction for the adjacent orange groves cuts the river's flow in daytime, but it recovers early evening. Barbel pay attention to this phenomenon. Directions: from

Estepona N340 west, exit north before Sotogrande. The N340 passes over the river itself. At Shell garage roundabout turn right, go for 2km to iron bridge over the river. From here you can see the sea barrier. Take a sharp left, double back 70m down a track under bridge to opposite bank at polo ground. A little further on is the swim. Gravel run 10 metres wide. Barbel to 4kg. Or try up the valley, at Sambana, or opposite Estación El Colmenar on the valley dam stretch, MA512.

Embalse de Depósito D1.1 (known as Barbel Lake to local expat anglers), free fishing, San Roque (carp, barbel, black bass). Carp to 9kg, gypsy barbel to 4kg in 2005. Luncheon meat works well here. Directions: N340 from Marbella to San Roque. Drive north past Estación San Roque over the level crossing for 1km to crossroads, two big *ventas* (inns) here. Left turn is for Los Barrios. You turn right along the scenic route for 2km to the big dam on your left. Park at the little workers' water plant and climb over the gate. The best fishing swims are nearest the road.

Embalse de Depósito DD1, aka **Embalse Los Barrios**, free fishing (carp, barbel). Barbel caught here to 11kgs in 2004. Directions: A381 to Los Barrios, then just to the south of town on the Río Guadarranque.

Embalse El Celemín, free fishing (barbel, carp, black bass). Generally cloudy water, barren shoreline with submerged dead trees in places. Level varies. Recreational areas for barbecues under shaded area with good pathways. You can drive right round this water. Directions: Cádiz, A381 east to Medina Sidonia, Then branch southeast on A393, then CA211 to Benalup de Sidonia. The lake is 4km east of Benalup.

Embalse de Barbate, a huge reservoir with free fishing but ask locally for details. Access is problematic. Directions: Cádiz, head east A381 to Alcalá de los Gazules. Lake is on southern boundary of town road all along main road.

Embalse de Bornos, Bornos, Río Guadalete, free fishing (carp, barbel and black bass). It's a big one. A pretty, family water where you can start the kids fishing right away. Up to 200 small carp were caught by three people in one session in 2002. Easy access, some litter problems by the town. Fish to the east of Bornos. Enter via the *embarcadero* (wharf). It's a bit deeper here. The far end has the deepest water of all. Several Spanish championships have been held here. Directions: from Jerez go northeast on A382 past Arcos to Bornos.

→ **When to fish?**

Visit during the week, when most waters are deserted. They become more crowded at weekends and on public holidays when water sports, including jet-skiing and swimming, take over.

↓ Seville

Oh Guadalquivir!
In Cazorla I saw you born
And today in Sanlúcar die.
A flash of clear water
Beneath a green pine
You were, and how happily you played.
Like me, close to the sea, river of brackish mud,
Do you dream of your beginnings?

Venerated poet Antonio Machado wrote these lines about the Río Guadalquivir, lifeblood of the Andalusian region. These days, because so much water is siphoned off for irrigation and human consumption, its flow is much reduced, affecting the fish population. In Moorish times the Atlantic species of sturgeon, which can grow to 3.5 metres and weigh 280 kilos, thrived in its waters. Every spring they used to migrate up the

river to spawn, travelling as far as Córdoba, 230 kilometres from the sea.

A caviar factory, which opened at Coria del Río, near Seville, in1930, processed 3,186 sturgeon between 1932 and 1954. But in the 1950s it closed (its heritage lives on in the name of a Coria angling club, El Esturión). Sadly, the caviar project coincided with a decline in fish numbers.

The construction of the Alcalá dam in 1932 restricted the breeding grounds to the lower Guadalquivir. Over the next 60 years they virtually disappeared due to deterioration in water quality and overfishing in the lower part of the estuary. The fish was protected by law in 1983 and put on the endangered list in 1986. Too late – the last one was caught at Seville in 1975, though there may still be a small population left in the Gulf of Cádiz.

In 1995-97 the Andalusian government launched a captive breeding programme with a view to re-introducing a sustainable sturgeon population in the Guadalquivir. Sturgeon are being bred in freshwater tanks at the Piscifactoría Sierra Nevada, Riofrío (Granada), and later transferred to a saltwater facility in Cádiz.

Licences: Delegación Provincial de Medio Ambiente: Avda. Innovación, s/n, Edificio. Minister, 41020. Sevilla. Tel: 955 004 400. Fax: 955 004 489. Email: delagada.se.cma@juntadeandalucia.es

Information: Manuel Pichardo Ortega, Federación Andaluza de Pesca Deportiva Sevilla, C/ Hytasa, 38, Edificio Toledo 1-4, módulo 7, 41006 Sevilla. Tel/Fax: 954 422 208, Mobile: 670 970 405. Email: sevilla@fapd. org; Asociación Deportiva Big Bass Alcalá, Apdo. 369, 41500 Alcalá de Guadaira (Sevilla).

Boat licences (21 euros per year including insurance): Confederación Hidrográfica del Guadalquivir, Comisaría de Aguas, Plaza de España, Sector 11, 41071 Sevilla. Tel: 954 939 400.

San Juan de Aznalfarache, Río Guadalquivir, free fishing (carp, barbel, bleak, big eels). Fish section between San Juan and Seville. Depth is 3-9 metres. Average width of channel is 100 metres. There is a lot of greenery by the bank. Directions: from Seville, Autovia 530 south, turn off for San Juan. Once there, head for Calle Betis and the river.
Darsena de Sevilla, Río Guadalquivir, Seville city centre, free fishing (carp, barbel, eels, tench, bass, sun fish, shad, bleak). The Darsena is the

river basin that diverts a channel from the Río Guadalquivir through the city centre. Average depth is 3-8 metres, up to 12 metres in the Lagos de España (port). The water level here varies when the sluice is opened for boats to reach the port. Two locations: an area around Puente del Alamillo (carrying the northern ring road) and from the sluice at the Pasarela de la Cartuja bridge down to the El Copero quarter. Directions: buy a city street map. Alamillo is at the north end of the Darsena. El Copero is down by the Puente del Quinto Centenario.

Paseo de la Barqueta, Seville city centre, Río Guadalquivir, and Lago Azul, free fishing (carp, barbel, eels, tench, perch and black bass). Average depth 3 to 4 metres. Fish next to the bridge Puente de la Barqueta. You can spot barbel here just under the surface, caught to 3kg and five in a session to 10kg. Carp pop up here as well. Recently 25 carp and barbel to 75kg were landed here in four hours. Fish for bass with a red spoon by the rushes at dusk. Sounds like heaven. Directions: middle of the city. Go to the Puente de la Barqueta. The embankment approach road is Calle del Torneo. Lago Azul is the port basin across the bridge.

> You can spot barbel just under the surface. Recently 25 carp and barbel to 75kg were landed here in four hours. Fish for bass with a red spoon by the rushes at dusk. Sounds like heaven.

Punta del Verde (Lago Sur), Río Guadalquivir, Seville city centre, free fishing (carp, barbel, bleak, eels, black bass, sea bass). Calm water without much current to 4-5 metres depth. Directions: fish downstream of the bridge Puente del Quinto Centenario in El Copero quarter. Road to El Copero runs along the embankment.

Coria del Río, Río Guadalquivir, free fishing (common and royal carp, crucian, sun fish, eels, bleak, nase and sea bass). Three zones to fish: 1. Start of path, to beginning of houses. A concrete embankment, comfortable fishing, channel is 30 metres wide here. Used by local clubs Sociedad de Pesca Cavra, and Club el Esturión; 2. From Bar Alforo to the wharf. Rarely used as the channel is only 3-4 metres wide here. From the wharf to the main channel it is good; 3. Río Pudio swims. Can be difficult to fish due to strong tidal currents. Try ledgering with earthworm, maggots, bread, crab and shrimp. Sweetcorn will attract carp to a good size. Popular seafood restaurants in town provide a welcome distraction. Directions: Seville ring road, SE30, exit to Coria (due south) by local highway, SE660. Follow the railway line to the junction of the old Coria highway, where the line stops. Take the first entrance towards Coria, go by this road for 1km. The Río Guadalquivir forms the right margin of the town for 2km.

Embalse José Torán, La Puebla de los Infantes, free fishing (royal and common carp, Iberian and common barbel, tench, nase, black bass, sun fish). Three metres deep in summer, 5-6 metres in winter. A lot of fish at Amigos del Guadalquivir rock, a bag of 33kg being landed here in three hours. Directions: from Seville go east on the A431, exit left at Lora del Río. Go north on SE147 and SE146 towards La Puebla. After passing the Ermita (hermitage), the dam is to your left.

Embalse de Torre del Águila, El Palmar de Troya, free fishing, navigable (royal and common carp, barbel, crucian, black bass, nase, hybrids). Easy access to the bank, easy to get to from Seville, easy to fish. Two fishing areas. Where you first arrive, go left towards the eucalyptus trees – it's deeper here. And from the eucalyptus trees to the dam. Here it is quite shallow, so fish at a distance. There are constant changes in the water level, as the dam irrigates local agriculture. It might be best in the spring. It's certainly better during the week when there is no one about.

Directions: take the A376 south from Seville to Utrera. Go south on the A364 to El Palmar de Troya. At town centre, turn right. Go a few km on an old road to a small crossing indicated by an old sign and small bridge. Go left and pass the dam spillway and small irrigation channel, for 1km. At the bankside there is a weekend bar and tap (water non-drinkable).

Alcalá de Guadaira, Río Guadaira, free fishing (carp, barbel, eels, pike). A smaller river set in a forest, where you can dream in peace. Crystalline water — you can see the fish three metres down. Big carp, up to 10kg. Eels up to 4.5kg. Pike population is on its way down. Can suffer local pollution but recovers quickly. Best spots are at la Comba, due to its good depth, and at Barriada La Liebre. Directions: from Seville drive east on the A92. Exit right after15km for Alcalá.

Embalse Puebla de Cazalla, Puebla de Cazalla, free fishing (carp, black bass). Very attractive spot, but difficult to get around the perimeter. So fish by the dam, just off the road. As there is little shade, take a brolly and loads of water. Directions: head east from Seville on the A92 towards Osuna. Exit for La Puebla de Cazalla. Continue south on SE452 to reach the dam.

Presa de Cantillana, Cantillana, Río Guadalquivir, free fishing (barbel, carp and bass). A 3kg bass was caught, on fly, by the dam – with a 20cm barbel still lodged in its throat. Stay quiet along the bank to locate carp and barbel at the margins. Cast directly to them. Directions: from Seville head east on the A431, exit at Cantillana. The dam is left through the town.

Embalse del Huesnar, Constantina and Cazalla, free fishing (carp, gypsy barbel, sun fish and black bass). A reservoir dating from the 1990s set in the Sierra Norte nature park, fed by the Huéznar river. Clear water and a very wide shoreline. Slight fishing pressure. Good for bass. Best spot for carp and barbel at the fishing platforms at the main tail-end of the water. Directions: take the A431 towards Córdoba. Exit at Lora del Río, head north for Constantina on A455, take the old road west to Pedroso. Dam is south, to the left.

Riviera de Huéznar, Tramo Medio (agency controlled river), free fishing (carp, barbel, black bass, trout). The Huéznar valley is a really beautiful area. Barbel, carp and black bass are caught up to the bridge at the Fábrica del Pedroso. Bass fishing good from the Fábrica. The whole locality is good for summer fishing.

Zone 1: From El Pedroso go east 1km and take the Constantina fork at the crossroads. Park on the small esplanade just before the bridge over the Huéznar river at the Jarosa recreational area. This section is a lake in spring, dwindling to a river in summer and autumn. An excellent spot for gypsy barbel. Zone 2. Right bank of reservoir. Easy access from the bridge via a pathway. There is 1km of flat shoreline. It is a good spot for carp. Zone 3. Below the bridge at Molina de Cestano. A good place to catch bass is where the river flows into the lake. Use Rapalas. Best in the evenings during spring and autumn. Go down past second zone, east to the bank. Here the shoreline is more difficult to traverse. It's not fished often and is very productive with artificial lures to bass. The shore is rocky with the odd submerged cork oak tree.

Embalse del Pintado, Guadalcanal, free fishing (carp, barbel, black bass). Water is situated at low altitude in a spur of the Sierra Morena, surrounded by cork oaks. In summer fish at the tail-end of the water by the Cuevas de Santiago. Take the Cazalla-Guadalcanal highway C432, then the Carretera de la Hoya de Sta. María. Park at the bridge where the road crosses the water. Fish here where the Benalija creek enters the main lake, or walk upstream where the barbel will take your fly in similar fashion. Excellent in early morning. Another spot is to the right of the dam, entering by El Cristo. Catch gypsy barbel here up to 4kg, on fly. Be careful not to spook the fish as you traverse the elevated walls. An effective substitute for specialist fly tackle is to use a plastic bubble with some flies attached to a couple of leaders dropped off the main line. Directions: go east from Seville on the A431, then north on A432 to Cazalla. Signposts indicate the water, due west about 10 km.

At Cazalla de la Sierra, stay at Posada del Moro, Paseo del Moro, s/n, on southern approach to town (Tel: 954 884 326, Fax: 954 884 858). Garden and pool. Cazalla is famous for its anise and cherry brandy. Sample the best brand in the Miura wine store, in a converted Franciscan church facing the market. Turismo, Paseo del Moro, 2, on road into town from south (tel: 954 883 562, www.skill.es/cartuja). Three kilometres east of Cazalla, off the A455 to Constantina, is the restored 500-year-old Cartuja monastery.

Almadén de la Plata, Río Viar, El Pedroso, free fishing (black bass, carp, barbel, sun fish, Iberian nase, pike, eels, algun). Beautiful scenery, deep holes for black bass and eddies for barbel. Both grow to spectacular sizes. Low water in summer. Best in spring. Nearby Río Calar also does well. Directions: from Seville go north, N630. Exit east at Sta. Olalla del Cala. Go 15km east to Almadén de la Plata. Follow A421 east to a ford.

Embalse de Cala, Lagos de Serrano, free fishing (carp, barbel, black bass). A very accessible area surrounded by villages, good restaurants and camping facilities. Boats allowed. Dam is at the irrigation plant. By now water should have recovered from pollution caused by farming practices. Directions: from Seville head north on the N630, exit at El Ronquillo and drive 10 km to the water, due east.

Alcalá del Río, Río Guadalquivir, free fishing (carp, barbel, black bass, eels, bleak). Fish near the dam, variable depth in both waters. Easier to catch barbel below the dam. Above, black bass are bigger and easier to catch. Directions: head north from Seville on A431 about 20km to Alcalá.

Embalse de la Minilla, Venta de Alto, free fishing (carp, barbel, black bass). A lot of big carp. Moderately clear and variable depth to over 4 metres. The other end to the dam (tail-end) is easier to fish and has more bass. Small inlets characterise this water. Excellent environment with good sport. The water is divided into three zones. Below the dam impressive Iberian barbel and numerous carp and large black bass are caught in the channel's pools. A great place for barbel fishing is at the tail zone where they come to spawn. There are carp here too. Most carp are commons or royals, but there are some with a tapered torpedo profile. Directions: from Seville about 45km. Head north on the N630, exit at Venta de Alto. The water is north of town to the left of the highway.

Embalse de Agrio, Aznalcóllar, free fishing (carp, barbel and black bass). Clear water. Consistently high water level even in summer. Goes deep to 10 metres. Sunken trees aplenty create the right environment for bass. They have grown big due to the introduction of red crayfish in the 1990s. Monstrous carp. A lot more to 5-6kg. At dusk, barbel (up to one metre long) will gather in large groups in shallow water by the margins. This lake has the biggest bird population in Seville province. Take care with the uneven banks. Accommodation at *casas rurales*, Tel: 955 750 981.

Directions: from Seville take the N431 west towards Huelva. Exit at Sanlúcar la Mayor. Cross the Río Guadiamar and take the local road north to Aznalcóllar. Go through town in direction of Castillo de las Guardas. It's 2km further to the dam. Before crossing the dam wall, turn left on the track running parallel to the right bank of the water. Park and foot it over the wall to the overflow area.

⬇ Huelva

Licences: Delegación Agencia Medio Ambiente, Sanlúcar de Barrameda, 3, 21071 Huelva. Tel: 959 011 500. Fax: 959 011 501. Email: delegado.hu.cma@juntadeandalucia.es

Boat licence: Confederación Hidrográfica del Guadiana, Comisaría de Aguas, C/Sinforiano Madronero, 12, 06011 Badajoz. Tel: 924 212 100. Email: chguadiana@mma.es www.chguadiana.es

Information: Francisco Sánchez García, Federación Andaluza de Pesca Deportiva, Avda Francisco Montenegro, s/n, 1 planta, (Real Club Marítimo de Huelva), 21001 Huelva. (postal address: Apartado de Correos 473, 21080 Huelva.) Tel & Fax: 959 261 448. For specialist advice, go to: www.geocities.com/basshuelva. Email: basshuelva@wanadoo.es

All directions given are from Huelva unless otherwise stated.

Embalse de Piedras, Cartaya, free fishing (shad, barbel, black bass and carp). In a beautiful location, big busy reservoir which provides clean water for the people of Huelva. It's possible to land 50 shad in a few hours averaging 0.3kg. Directions: west N431 from Huelva. Exit at Cartaya, take the road to Tariquejos, then turn on to a worn road for the dam wall.

Embalse de San Bartolomé de la Torre, free fishing (carp and black bass). A small lake with level banks and an average depth of 12 metres. Surrounded by quiet, pleasant woodland. There is easy access direct from the road. Directions: north N431, northwest A495 to San Bartolomé. Now go north towards Alosno for 1km. The water is nearby.

Embalse de El Picote, El Almendro, free fishing (black bass and carp). Many submerged trees provide an excellent habitat for the introduced bass stockfish. Small when introduced, but growing. Directions: north N431 via Gibraleón, northwest A495 past San Bartolomé towards El Almendro. The lake is to the east of town. Access is via a 3km private dirt track in good condition. Look out for signs for the dirt track (*pista de tierra*) for Alonso and Satiendo de Alonso. As you drive through, ask the owners not to lock the gate in the evening so you can get out.

Embalse de Chanza, El Granado, free fishing (black bass, carp and barbel). Submerged white town is a good spot for bass. Reputedly to 4kg. No boats are permitted and fishing from the bank can be difficult. Directions: on the Portuguese border about 70km from Huelva. Northwest on N431 and A495 past San Bartolomé to El Granado. Then the Carretera de la Confederación Hidrográfica del Guadiana to the *embalse*.

Valverde del Camino, Beas and Valverde del Camino, free fishing (black bass and carp). A small water that goes very deep and is 80 per cent full all year. Best to fish April-September. Fishing from the bank is not ideal. By boat there are four or five good spots at the tail and by the island. This is the bass hot spot, at the tail-end of the reservoir. Casting by the El Campanario (bell tower) is recommended. Carp landed here of 15kg. For carp "as big as horses", try near the dam wall. Directions: north E1, N435 to Valverde. From here go via the Cruce de Calañas. It is 0.5km to the track.

Embalse del Zumajo, Minas de Riotinto, free fishing (carp, black bass and barbel). A shallow lake in pretty surroundings. Rent boats and canoes from the Bar Puerto Zumajo. The local angling club is San José

(Riotinto), C/Santa Bárbara, 22, Minas de Riotinto 21660. Directions: north N435, exit east for Riotinto and take the road to Nerva. Along the way, turn off south for Las Delgadas (signposted to the lake). The lake should be to your right, opposite Monte Sorromero.

Embalse de Zufre, Zufre, free fishing (carp, barbel, bogas (Iberian nase), sun fish and black bass). A deep lake (average depth 3-4 metres) of medium size set in the beautiful landscape of the Sierra de Aracena and Picos de Aroche. A unique characteristic of the Zufre barbel is that its belly is fatter than those found elsewhere. They shun artificial lures. One of the best baits is crayfish that can be found in shallow holes by the bank. Fishing pressure is light here because the water is fenced in. Black bass average weight is 1kg but they go to 3kg. Gypsy barbel exceed 4kg and are also found in the Guillena, Gergal, Minilla, Chanza, and Cora La Mora reservoirs.

The terrain has good variety. There are beaches, islands, steps, and hundreds of rarely visited inlets. The lake supplies Seville with its drinking water so the quality is consistently good. It is between the reservoirs La Minilla and Aracena and is served by the Guadalquivir water authority. They all share the same tributary, La Rivera de Huelva.

Directions: Getting to the water is not a problem. Easiest access is from Seville, N630 north, exit left on N433 towards Aracena, right on A461 to Zufre. Go east on the Carretera de la Dehesa La Noria, a short distance to the reservoir. Reaching the fishing platforms is a little harder as cattle fencing can make access difficult. When you arrive at Zufre village there are two options: 1. Take the first turning to the reservoir for the road that borders the water and crosses the tail-end via a bridge. Leave your vehicle by the road and foot it down to the bank. 2. Take the second turning, 200 metres further up the road from the first. Look for the Dehesa La Noria and follow this old road.

Embalse de Aracena, Corte Concepción, free fishing (carp). Carp to a good size are caught on sweetcorn. *"Ganado Bravo"*. Bearing in mind the type of cows they breed in this part of the world the warning signs seem appropriate. Directions: north N435, east N433. After Aracena exit north for Corte Concepción. The lake is northeast of here.

Embalse de Guillena, El Ronquillo and Castiblanco de los Arroyos, free fishing (carp and barbel). A paradise for barbel. Penultimate dam in a network of reservoirs supplying water for the Confederación Hidrográfica del Guadalquivir. This water system includes Aracena,

Zufre, Cala, La Minilla, and El Gergal. Water ends up via the Algaba reservoir in the Río Guadalquivir. Nearby waters include Ronquillo and Castilblanco de los Arroyos. They are all fed in part by the Rivera de Huelva.

Built in the early 1970s, it is always full. At the first sign of rain it has to open its sluice gate. One dam up is the Embalse de Cala. It produces hydro power for Seville and will affect the water level at Guillena every day and fish behaviour. Its level changes by two metres in 12 hours. You may be left high and dry, so fish to the average level in the deeper parts. Directions: From Seville, N630 north, exit on A460 to Guillena, then 14km on a rock'n'roll road over the mountains before descending to the dam.

Embalse Jarrama, Nerva, free fishing (carp, barbel and black bass). A new lake so few anglers visit at present. Good water for black bass. The surroundings are nicely set off with pines, white rock roses and bullrushes. In Nerva there are tackle shops, restaurants, hotels, camping and bars.

Directions: north N435, exit east for Nerva. From the tourist office in Nerva, located at the town exit for Seville, head in direction of Seville for 3.5 km then take a small track to the right of the main road. Go another 3.5 km to the tail-end of the lake. For the dam wall, exit town in direction of Seville on the old highway towards El Madroño for 5 km till you pass a garage dump on your right. Take a left down a track before a bridge and drive for 2km, the dam wall will come into view. The road is unsurfaced but ok.

Embalse de Sillilo, Valverde del Camino, free fishing (carp, barbel and black bass). Pretty, but no natural shade. Two to three metres deep, the peculiar water is the colour of the surrounding hills. Before pegging up have a good breakfast in nearby Valverde. Directions: north N435 to Valverde. Now from the highway turn off pass by the cemetery to a narrow road. The dam is next to an old chimney, which can be seen from a distance.

Pantano de Candón, Candón, free fishing (carp and barbel). A very pretty lake, it is small and deep with level banks and a sandstone bottom. The carp average one kilo, and there are good restaurants nearby. Directions: east A92 to Niebla, then exit northwest to Candón. The water is to the east of town.

Pantano del Corumbel, La Palma del Condado, free fishing (carp, sun fish and barbel). A muddy bottom with submerged rock roses and hence cloudy water. Black bass population hasn't recovered from low water in 2002. The carp are of no great reputation. But the barbel grow to huge sizes. Boats are permitted. A channel of the old river is submerged in the middle at the tail-end of the lake — find fish here. Two options: By boat, look for other swims in inlets before getting to the dam wall. Go past here 20 to 30 metres to deep borders of first section and deep borders by the drowned eucalyptus trees; or cross old roads to the right of the lake on earth tracks which all lead bankside. Directions: east A472 to La Palma del Condado. Take the new road north in the direction of Berrocal. Drive for 4 km till you reach the water.

Embalse del Calabazar, Sotiel Coronada, free fishing (carp, barbel, black bass). There are many inlets and an island by the dam. The lake has steep sides and access is difficult from the bank. Boats are banned. As a result, few bother to fish here. The barbel are many and exceed 10kg, the carp are fewer but grow large. Directions: North on N435 to Valverde del Camino then A493 northwest. Before arriving at Calañas turn left past village of Sotiel Coronada for lake.

Barbel in Spain

Six species found in Spain have closer genetic ties with the Caucasus, Greece and Middle East than Europe. These are the *Barbus comizo, Barbus bocagei, Barbus microcephalus, Barbus sclateri, Barbus guiraonis* and *Barbus grallsi*. Sharing closer genetic ties with other European species are members of a sub-genetic order, the *Barbus haasi* and the *Barbus meridionales*. Usually, there is a clear-cut geographical distribution of barbel species according to river systems.

The Iberian barbel (*barbo comizo: Barbus comizo*) grows to the largest size (note: English names are used here, followed by the Spanish then generic titles). Its snout is longer than other Iberian barbel species. On bigger specimens the head is huge. Varies from dark to light green in colour. It can be found in water systems from the Atlantic coast to the west part of Castilla-La Mancha, in the rivers Guadiana and Guadalquivir. In remote parts of Extremadura, it is a cult fish, growing to 15-18 kilos. Its numbers have declined significantly in the lower reaches of the major river basins. →

→ In the same waters as the *comizo* are found the small-head barbel (*barbo cabecicorto: Barbus microcephalus*) and the snouted Iberian barbel (*barbo común: Barbus bocagei*). In Spain the latter is known as the common barbel. It is also found in the Río Júcar. It's more abundant in Portugal where it is called the barbo do Norte. Both these species grow to 12 kilos, but the former is now quite scarce.

The gypsy barbel (*barbo gitano: Barbus sclateri*), a sub-species of the snouted Iberian barbel, is sometimes called the Andalusian barbel (yes, it's found around Andalusia). It is canary-yellow or orange from the lateral line down. It is found in the Río Rumblar at Jaén for example, and the Río Segura to the east. Average caught weights are between three and five kilos and 10-kilo specimens are not unheard-of. The record is 14kg. Catch gypsy barbel in the reservoirs Zufre (separate sub-species found here), Guillena, Gergal, Minilla, Chanza, and Cora La Mora.

Want to catch one? If there are a lot of crayfish in the water, use very hard boilies to deter them.

Grael's barbel (*Barbus graellsii*), also a sub-species of the snouted Iberian, is found all along the Río Ebro basin and in the Ter and Llobregat rivers.

The Mediterranean barbel has two sub-species. *Barbo de montaña* (*Barbus meridionalis*) can be caught from the eastern half of Castilla-La Mancha to the Mediterranean coast. It grows to 11 kilos, recorded catch. Try the Palància, Turia and Xúquer rivers. *Barbo del mediterráneo* (*Barbus guiraonis*) is caught in the Muga, Huvia, Ter and Bèsos rivers.

The *Barbo de cola roja* (*Barbus haasi*) is very scarce and possibly extinct in Spain. It used to be caught in the Llobregat, Ebro, Francoli, Palància, Túria and Mijares (upstream channels). A Medio Ambiente report in 2000 claimed that proposed dam construction at Salto de Jánovas in Huesca province would probably deal the deathblow.

Want to catch one? If there are a lot of crayfish in the water, use very hard boilies to deter them. Guess which flavour works well? Yes, crayfish. Catch barbel on the bottom, using sweetcorn. A triple rig is the way to go. Two strings are baited normally, the third being fitted with foam to make it buoyant. This is a killer rig for carp as well.

When the barbel's regular natural food, i.e. crayfish, is scarce, catch them on small livebait, pike rig style. Believe it or not, many large specimens have been caught using a fly. Go to the Río Grande in the Málaga section for advice on this method. You won't necessarily require game tackle.

⬇ Córdoba

In the time of the Moors, the Guadalquivir (the Wadi al-Kabir, or "Great River") was a more powerful river with a stronger current. Water mills lined the banks to provide the city with water. A restored example is located below Córdoba's Moorish fortresss, the Alcázar. Up to the time of Columbus the river was still navigable by ocean-going ships. From the multi-arched Puente Romano (Roman bridge), built in the time of Julius Caesar, you get a great view of the superb mosque.

Licences: Delegación Agencia Medio Ambiente, Comisaría de Aguas, C/Tomás de Aquino, s/n. (Edificio Servicios Múltiples), 7a Planta, 14071 Córdoba. Tel: 957 001 300. Fax: 957 239 014. Email: delegado.co.cma@juntadeandalucia.es

Information: Manuel Silva Pérez, Federación Andaluza de Pesca Deportiva, Carbonell y Morad, 9, 14001 Córdoba. Tel, 957 478 990. Fax: 957 478 990. Mobile: 670 974 222. Email: cordoba@fapd.org Specialist advice: www.basscordoba.com and email: basscordoba@supercable.es

All directions are from Córdoba unless otherwise stated.

Embalse de la Brena, Almodóvar del Río, free fishing (carp, barbel, black bass). Nice scenery. Sweetcorn and worm for the carp and barbel. Boats are permitted. The boat launch belongs to the nautical club. Directions: west on A431 to Almodóvar. Turn right under the main road for the lake to the north of town. Bad access for vehicles. A better entrance: pass the dam wall and continue on the dirt road until you reach El Chiringuito. From here you may need a four-wheel-drive.

Embalse del Retortillo, Río Retortillo, Puebla de los Infantes, free fishing with special regulations (carp and barbel). Easy access for car. Crystal clear waters. Mostly royal and common carp to 3kg at La Peña de la Campana. Loads of big barbel and carp on the left bank where the Ciudadeja and Retortillo rivers enter the reservoir. Directions: from Seville drive east A431, exit at Peñaflor. Go north to La Puebla de los Infantes, then north 8km out of town on SE141 to the reservoir.

Embalse de Guadanuño, Cerro Muriano, free fishing (carp, barbel, black bass and pumpkinseed). A calm place, with good access to the shoreline and 75 per cent of the swims accessible from the bankside. This is a clean lake of medium depth. The water can be a technical fish as the carp are a bit canny. The surroundings make up for this. They are clean and quiet. The best time is May when it's easier to catch fish. Baits to use include maggots, bread and sweetcorn. There are some big carp. Directions: north on N432. The highway bypasses Cerro Muriano. Take a right towards Estación de Obejo. Take a left towards the lake. Entrance to the lake is by the dam wall.

Embalse de Las Jaras, Villaviciosa, free fishing (carp, barbel, black bass and pumpkinseed). A small pretty clear lake in a nice setting with variable depth. This is a good water for bass (big ones to 3kg) and plenty of smaller chaps. The bankside has good cover for them, bullrushes and submerged trees. The carp grow large. A 10kg specimen was landed in 2002 on boilies. They grow to 18kg. The mornings are very productive. Barbel are caught to 5kg. There are some big pumpkinseed and a few trout. Use strong line as there is a snaggy bottom. This is a popular water, hence the litter problem. Directions: just north of Córdoba, in the hills. Take Avenida del Brillante out of the city, heading towards the Parque Los Villares, and C110 towards Villaviciosa.

Embalse de Puente Nuevo, Villaviciosa, free fishing (black bass, carp, barbel and pike). A very deep lake. There are many black bass, some approaching the Spanish record. February is the best month. It's too hot in summer. Pike are not common, but some to 10kg have been landed. Carp can be found near the dam wall. The barbel go like a train. Both are fewer in number than before. They can be found at the thermal power station, where hot water is discharged into the lake, and at the Bejarano stream by La Espada gorge. Boats are permitted here since fishing from the bank can be a problem. Directions: north N432, after 30 km exit west A433 towards Villaviciosa. The water is to the right of the road.

Embalse de Santa María, Pozoblanco, day ticket (carp, common and royal, Iberian nase, barbel and tench). A family spot. Small water in pleasant surroundings with lots of oaks. Very clean. The kids will have no difficulty in catching fish here. It's good for tench. Purchase day tickets within the lake perimeter or at the lake bar. There are also cafes, restaurants, bakery, barbecue area and a children's playground. Next door is a golf course and riding club. This water is the home of the Club de Pesca Deportiva Pozoblanco. Permission to fish can also be obtained from the Pozoblanco town hall (*ayuntamiento*). Directions: go north on N432, exit north N502 at Espiel. Exit east AC420 at Alcaracejos, for Pozoblanco.

Embalse San Pedro, Fuente Ovejuna, free fishing (carp and barbel). Cloudy water, shallow at the dam wall to three metres deep. Many spots to fish from the nice even bank. There are 50 pegs. Directions: north on N432. After Peñarroya and before Fuente Ovejuna take a right to the village of El Porvenir de la Industria (the future of industry).

Embalse de Sierra Boyera, Belmez and Peñarroya, free fishing (black bass, carp, barbel, and sun fish). Quiet, many tributaries, different depth, no boats allowed. There is excellent access to all parts of the water. Good for bass at bridge by the tail-end of the lake. There are carp here to 5kg and many more, smaller fish to 1.5kg. Barbel are caught up to 3kg on potato. Iberian nases are best caught in the winter. There is not much weed. The sun fish (*perca sol*) are many and annoying. Directions: north N432 to Peñarroya, the lake is just to the south of town.

Río Guadalquivir, Alcolea, free fishing (carp, barbel, Iberian nase, black bass, pike and sun fish). One of the prettiest rivers in Spain. The average depth is two metres. Good current and easy access to comfortable fishing. Forty fish to 20kg are a common catch. Carp averaging a kilo make up 80 per cent of the bag. A good barbel spot is to the east of Alcolea by the bridge near the railway line. There are three zones to fish: 1. Guadalbarbo; 2. Las Quemadas, just before Alcolea turn right off the main road to the river; 3. Carbonell. Directions: just east of the city. Follow minor road north of river to Alcolea or take autoroute NIV and within minutes exit left for Alcolea.

Embalse de San Rafael de Navallana, Ríos Guadalmellato and Guadalquivir, Alcolea, free fishing (black bass, barbel, carp, common and royal, crucian, sun fish and pike). Famous for its bass. As good from the bank as from the boat. Built in 1969, situated south of the Embalse Guadalmellato. Clean and deep with thick bankside vegetation. The good-quality water comes from the Sierra Morena a via the Guadalbarbo, Varas and Cuza rivers. A lot of submerged trees and rock roses provide an ideal habitat for the dominant bass population. The carp have increased recently in size and number and are quite large.

There are two zones divided by the highway viaduct: 1. Towards the Guadalmellato dam. Best here for good pike to 12kg and bass. There are lots of barbel. No livebaiting allowed. For bass, use surface lures at dusk. The water is no good for deep-water spinning because of underwater obstacles and trees breaking the surface. The bass go deep in January, July and August, so fish at zone 2; 2. This is towards the San Rafael Navallana dam, is the most popular end and has the deepest, clearest water.

For pike fish at El Cazador and at Embalse de Villafranco. A lot of smaller ones are caught on red and silver spoons. For bass go to La Isla, Los Cortados and La Ametralladora by the Civil War bunker. A favourite Rapala is the Fat Rap San, perch colour, green on the back, dark orange or yellow on the belly. It's best retrieved at 2-3 metres depth. Bass are caught mainly from the boat jetty. Favourite Spanish lures are vinyls. Boats are permitted. Spring and autumn are the best times to visit.

The bass fishing, once exceptional, has now declined a little. Some put this down to the extermination of their natural food source the crab, by Medio Ambiente, because they were eating into the dam wall foundations. A likely story! However, this remains a popular (over-fished?) venue. It must still be good.

Directions: east NIV/E5 to Alcolea turn-off, then to the dam road, northeast of Alcolea. After the Roman bridge, turn right and the dam is 2km up the road and 3km further on is a viaduct that crosses the town dam and divides the water. A boat can be launched from the slipways for both waters, to each side of the viaduct. Where to stay? Near the dam at Km393, old Carretera de Madrid, is La Hostal La Lancha, tel: 957 320149.

Embalse de Guadalmellato, Río Guadalmellato, Alcolea, free fishing (carp, barbel, black bass and pike). Set in the Sierra Cordobesa, it is up to 70 metres deep. No boats are allowed and the access road is a little hairy. Some say it's better at Rafael de Navallana, as the clear water makes spinning difficult. Carp fishing is good at the dam wall using sweetcorn. Possibility of big solitary pike. Good fishing at zone 8km before the dam wall and at mouth of Río Varas. Three anglers landed 50 bass here in August, 2002. Directions: east NIV/E5 exit at Alcolea, now go north 10 km to the lake.

Embalse Minicentral, Pedro Abad, free fishing (carp, Iberian nase and barbel). Easy access. A small dam for the mini-power station. There are big carp around the dam wall. Smaller barbel and Iberian nase exist in the current. Go downstream after the floodgates for a change. Baits successful here are masilla, sweetcorn and earthworm. Directions: east NIV/E5 to Pedro Abad, take CO402 towards Ademuz. The lake is just out of town.

Embalse de Yeguas, Cardeña and Villa del Río, free fishing (carp and barbel). Set in the Parque Natural de la Sierra de Cardeña y Montoro. Clear water to 7 metres depth. There is easy access to the shore. The banks are gravel with olive trees as a backdrop. Bass will take all artificial lures. The water level is very variable. In the summer this is a tourist spot. Directions: NIV/E5 east, exit at Villa del Río, then north towards Cardeña. Along the way turn off east on A420 for the water. Pantano Cordobilla, Badolatosa and Jauja, free fishing (carp, black bass and Iberian nase). A lot of red crab. Directions: south NIV/E5, then N331 towards Antequera. Just before Lucena exit west A340 for a few kms then minor roads southwest, to Jauja. Badolatosa is over the bridge on the west shore.

Embalse de Iznájar, Río Genil, Iznájar, free fishing (crucian, black bass, trout and sun fish). This huge water is the biggest reservoir in Andalusia. A crisis occurred in the summer of 2005 when the water was found to contain herbicide, used to spray olive trees in the area, and people in 22 municipalities were advised it was dangerous to drink. The effect on the fish was not immediately known, but it would be a brave, or foolish, man who ate anything hooked here until emergency measures and future rains clear up the problem. The bass, down in numbers due to the introduction of pumpkinseed, are a little cunning having got used to the decoys used by the locals. Normally, the fishing is good in October and November. The zone of the Río Sickle is good, where it enters the reservoir. Carp are plentiful and are best caught in autumn when feeding up for winter. Directions: south NIV/E5, N331 to Encinas Reales, exit east to Cuevas de San Marcos. You arrive at the top of the water. The town of Iznájar, at the centre of the lake, is 6km around the south shore. From San Marcos head north and east towards Rute for the north shore. You can also access the lake going north near Loja from the A92, the Granada-Antequera highway.

⬇ Jaén

Licences: Delegación Provincial de Medio Ambiente, C/ Fuente de Serbo, 3, 23071. Jaén. Tel: 953 012 400. Fax: 953 012 508. Email: Delegado.ja.cma@juntadeandalucia.es

Information: César Albusac Amador, Federación Andaluza de Pesca Deportiva, Lazo, 19, 23485 Pozo Alcón (Jaén). Tel: 953 738 729. Email: jaen@fapd.org. www.fapdjaen.com

Directions given are from Jaén unless otherwise stated.

Presa de San Julián, Río Guadalquivir, Andújar, free fishing (carp and barbel). Many carp and barbel. Cloudy water when the dam is opened. Quiet, with few anglers. Directions: north N323 to Bailén, west NIV/E5; go 15 km past Andújar, turn off north and right for San Julián. Next to the Río Guadalquivir.

Embalse de El Encinarejo, Río Jándula, Andújar, free fishing (carp and barbel). Stable water level all year around. Clear water, sandy bottom and large, semi-submerged granite rocks. Abundance of weed between the rocks. Very pretty environment. Cork oaks and white rock roses around the shore. This water has a good reputation for large carp and bass, 15 carp from 6-14kg being landed over two sessions in 2000. Use translucent vinyl lures of any colour to catch bass near the bank to 30-60cm in length. Try wobblers and poppers, worms, moved slowly along the surface to catch bass to 3kg. Small to medium bass are located by the dam wall. Bigger ones have become rare due to over-fishing at this popular mark. Here there are massive carp which are ignored by the locals. The lake is always full, since it is below the Embalse de Jándula and the water is cooler. The left bank is deepest. Boats are permitted.

Directions: north on N323 to Bailén, west NIV/E5, exit at Andújar, take road north towards the Santuario de la Virgen de la Cabeza and Puertollano. Cross the metal bridge over the Río Jándula and turn right along a forest track 2km to the dam wall. Go up the hill into the recreational area, where there are a couple of spots to launch your boat from.

Embalse del Jándula, Andújar, free fishing (carp, barbel, Iberian nase and black bass). Located in the Sierra Morena, in surroundings of great beauty and ecological value. Steep banks, but very deep, 25 metres maximum. A lot of submerged trees. When full, the lake provides a good bass habitat, some approaching the Spanish record (3kg) on a regular basis. Catching them is another matter. The easiest time is in April, May and June. Carp go to 10kg and there are plenty of good size barbel. Boilies attract the biggest specimens.

Directions: north on N323 to Bailén, west NIV/E5, exit at Andújar, take road north towards Puertollano to Santuario de la Virgen de la Cabeza. Pass the restaurant Los Pinos, go straight then turn right for Los Escoriales and the Presa Jándula. Continue to another turning for the dam.

Embalse del Rumblar, Río Rumblar, Baños de la Encina, free fishing (Iberian nase and carp). Variable depth. Clean water in a mountainous location. A lot of Iberian nase and some pike. Directions: north N323 to Bailén, northeast 4km on NIV, then left to Baños de la Encina. The reservoir is a few km to the northwest of town.

Embalse de Zocueca, Río Rumblar, Bailén, free fishing (black bass, pike and carp). Maximum depth 10 metres. The dam is regulated so there is a constant water level. There are big carp here. Directions: north N323 to Bailén, west NIV/E5 a few km to Zocueca. The reservoir is north of Zocueca.

Embalse de la Fernandina (also known as Embalse de Panzacola), La Carolina, free fishing (black bass, carp and pike). Famous for its pike. *Perca sol* (sun fish) were caught in 2001 for the first time. A quiet lake with good access. Shallow margins, although there are areas that are deep quite close in to the bank. There is a lot of weed everywhere. Plenty of carp and pike averaging 2-5kg, many to 5-8kg and catch recorded of 15kg. They are quite lithe in appearance. Some say it is better at Cijara. The Pantano de Panzacola is normally filled up. It's good for bass here. Go from Carolina. Directions: north N323, NIV/E5 to La Carolina. Exit east A301 towards Vilches, the road crosses the water a little further on. Go over the bridge, shortly after there is a track down to a small inlet of the reservoir. There is a village by the lake. Look out for a tall chimney by the shore in front of a big hill.

Embalse del Guadalén, Vilches and Arquillos, free fishing (carp, pike and black bass). Surrounded by olives, good for carp although no large bags, 80 smaller ones in one recent session. Guadalén has some nice restaurants. The Embalse de Fernandina is close by. Directions: north N323 to Bailén, east N322, exit at Linares, then north A312. Head towards Vilches for west bank, or Arquillos for east.

Embalse de Giribaile, Canena, free fishing (carp, common and royals, Iberian nase and black bass). A new, quiet, clean water set in farmland. The banks can get muddy. Few visitors. No boats are allowed. Access to the tail-end of the water can get difficult due to overgrown paths. The bass, generally small stock-fish, only takes a year or two to reach championship weight. La Fernandina is said to be much better for black bass. Newly introduced young fish were due to have matured by 2003. Two zones. The high zone is from Cortijo Las Norias to Cortijo del Ventanaje Bajo, via the Ariza Roman bridge. Directions: northeast A316 to Úbeda, west on N322 to Canena. From there, go north on the Carretera de la Presa. Take a track through the olive trees to the shoreline. This way may become difficult after rain. So try alternative tracks.

Arroyo del Ojanco, Río Guadalimar, free fishing (carp, Iberian nases and barbel). A clean shallow water. Mostly barbel, to 2.5kg. Variable depth. Directions: northeast A316 to Úbeda, then N322 towards Albacete, pass Villacarrillo, and after another 26km you reach Arroyo del Ojanco.

Embalse de Guadalmena, Río Guadalmena, Arroyo del Ojanco, free fishing (pike, black bass and carp). A clean water with variable depth. Set in mountains, it is very pretty with wild boar and deer. A lot of big pike and many bass to all sizes. Spring is best. If you can't catch the bass, go for the pike, always a banker. Carp to 20kg have been landed.

Pike to 7kg are commonplace. Boats are permitted, but there is poor access to the dam wall. Directions: northeast A316 to Úbeda, then N322 towards Albacete, pass Villacarrillo and after another 26km you reach Arroyo del Ojanco. Continue 4km, then go north on the Carretera del Condado for reservoir.

Embalse del Tranco, El Tranco and Cazorla, free fishing (rainbow trout, crucian and black bass). A nice setting in the Natural Park of Cazorla, Segura and Las Villas. Usually 40 per cent of capacity, but this is ok. Forty carp to 2kg, and two barbel to 3.5kg fell to maggots and sweetcorn in July, 2000, and in June 2002 a 5.6kg barbel was landed. Spot fish where the *pedalos* are rented out. Trout have escaped from the farm at Río Borosa and Río Aguamula. Locals have eaten most of the trout. There are many campsites to choose from. At the turning for the campsite Llanos de Arance, take the track to the water. It's a rough ride with many potholes. But it's passable.

To obtain permission to fish for trout in the designated coto areas, contact the Oficina del Parque Natural in Cazorla (Martínez Falero, 11. Tel: 953 720 125). Or purchase a ticket on site.

Directions: east A316 to Úbeda, then northeast on N322. For the southern end of the lake, exit the N322 at Torreperogil, taking A 315 southeast to Peal de Becerro, then A319 east to Cazorla. The A319 continues from Cazorla, enters the natural park and runs along the west side of the reservoir. Or exit the N322 at Villanueva del Arzobispo on narrow road to the Tranco dam. Or exit further east for Beas de Segura, turning south on A317 to El Tranco.

Embalse de Vadomojón (Río Víboras), Los Noguerones and Las Casillas, free fishing (carp, common and royal, black bass, rainbow trout and barbel). Clear, unobstructed water to 10 metres in depth surrounded by olives. The Víboras river flows from the Embalse de Víboras into Vadomojón. Shortly before the lake there is a union of the Río San Juan and the Arroyo Salado. Catch rainbow trout from these feeder rivers. Black bass to 1.5kg. Directions: southwest on A316, turning right shortly before Alcaudete. The only sealed approach road is on the left bank below the tail-end of the Río Víboras. Enter the centre of Los Noguerones and cross a bridge over the Río Víboras then towards the reservoir.

Extremadura

CHAPTER SIX

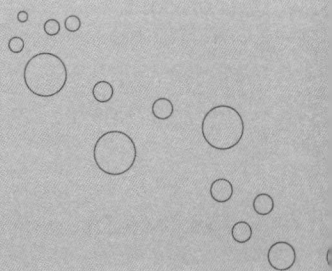

Extremadura, bordering Portugal, is one of Spain's least developed and least populated regions. Its two provinces, Badajoz in the south and Cáceres to the north, offer good opportunities for the angler.

⬇ Badajoz

Licences: Servicio Territorial de la Consejería de Obras Públicas, Urbanismo y Medio Ambiente, Avda. de Europa, 10, Badajoz. Tel: 924 011 000. Email: sca@aym.juntaex.es; Dirección General de Medio Ambiente, Servicio de Conservación de la Naturaleza, Avda. Portugal s/n, 06800 Mérida (Badajoz). Tel: 924 002 000, 924 382 861. www.mma.es

Information: José Fuentes Manchado, Federación Extremeña de Pesca, Travesía de Parejo, 9-4D, 06800 Mérida. Tel: 924 317 636. Email: fedextpesca@wanadoo.es. More information: For good pictures and maps of this region's *embalses* visit www.utepresasjuntaextre. com/. Click on "*Niveles actuales de embalses*"– a page pops up with daily water levels. For general information try www.juntaex.es and for accommodation www.extremadura.com

Boat licences: Confederación Hidrográfica del Guadiana, C/ Sinforiano Medrõnero, 12, 06001 Badajoz. Tel: 924 212 100. Email: chguadiana@mmma.es. www.chguadiana.es has excellent maps for the region.

The Río Guadiana cuts right through Badajoz. The Amigos del Guadiana are lobbying the city council for the construction of 100 *pesquils* (fishing platforms) around the city to create a competition-angling venue. Puerto la Bargueta de Sevilla and Mérida already have these facilities along their banks. Contact the Amigos through José Silgo Calzo, La Sociedad de Pescadores, Restaurante La Granadilla, C/Francisco Guerra, 6, 06011 Badajoz. Tel: 924 248 106.

Bass fans can contact the angling club Guadiana Bass Masters, Camino de La Guija, 23, Bloque Al, Puerta 3-1, 13005 Ciudad Real. Tel: 926 219 014. Email: guadianabassmaster@wanadoo.es

Sociedad Deportiva Puente Ajuda hold regular competitions that are open to all. They meet at the Bar El Rincón, C/República Argentina, in Badajoz.

Extremadura has a three-rod limit. All directions are given for a start at Badajoz.

Charca de Galgos, Esparragalejo, day ticket (tench). Open May 1-October 15. For tickets: Bar Pacha, C/Virgen de la Salud, 15, Esparragalejo. Directions: east A5 towards Mérida, northeast on sideroads to Esparragalejo.

Embalse de Proserpina, Mérida, club water (carp, tench, black bass, pumpkinseed). Best in April and May. The water is cloudy and there is an explosion of weed during the summer but goes by October. Good-size bass, averaging half a kilo. Fish vinyls with worm, size 15-20cm. Try watermelon-colour Rapalas, 7-11cm in size. Big royal and common carp average 6-9kg, one of 23kg caught in 2002. Sweetcorn is recommended here. There are thousands of sunfish and crayfish. For permission: three clubs in Mérida, addresses: C/Morerio de Vorgas, C/Enrique Sánchez de León, 83, and C/Almendralejo, 48. Directions: east A5/E90 to Mérida. Just north of the city.

Embalse de Cornalvo, Mérida, day ticket (carp). Very good for carp and bass, barbel ok. A pretty spot that is popular at the weekend. Directions: east A5 past Mérida to San Pedro, then local roads north to the lake.

Embalse de Valverde, Valverde de Mérida, day ticket (carp). Water is set in a wonderful natural environment. Open from the first weekend in May to October 15, except public holidays. For tickets: Bar la Gamba, Plaza de la Iglesia, Valverde. Directions: east A5 to Mérida, then side road east to Valverde.

Embalse de Alange, Mérida, free fishing (carp, barbel, black bass, pike, sun fish). Not many pike but they are big 'uns. From the dam, the left bank is where the Sau and Palomilles streams enter the reservoir. The bank is a bit rocky with stone fences and submerged trees, making it a good environment for bass. Access is good on the road from Alange towards Palomas.

The right bank is where the Río Valdemente enters the water. Here the shoreline is sandy and flat, making it a good spot for carp fishing. Access is via the road from Almendralejo. The central zone is where the Río Matachel arrives at the lake. It's good here for carp and barbel. The zone by the dam is reputedly the best all-year round spot for bass. From the boat spin for bass around the island that divides the water.

But watch out for the river currents as they can sweep your craft on to rocks. Directions: east A5/E90 to Mérida, bypass Mérida, south on A66, then exit east to Alange.

Embalse de Los Canchales, Los Canchales and Montijo (carp). For tickets: go to Cafetería Martín at La Garrovilla. Directions: take EX209 east to Montijo then the road north towards La Nava de Santiago. A tall antenna stands near the reservoir.

Embalse de Horno Tejero, Cordobilla de Lácara, day ticket (pike, black bass). A very pretty spot with clear water, level banks and it goes deep. Some good pike, bass to 3kg and many more to 2kg. Most around 15cm. Two places for bass: 1. Open water by the dam. 2. Sheltered roots of eucalyptus trees. Catch them on Rapalas and teaspoons. Try a streamer when your poppers stop working. For tickets: Bar El Cazador, Cordobilla. Directions: northeast on EX100 to La Roca de la Sierra, then east on local roads to La Nava de Santiago, then north to Cordobilla de Lácara. Horno Tejero is to the north.

Embalse del Boquerón, Cordobilla de Lácara, day ticket (carp, black bass). For tickets: Bar El Cazador, Cordobilla de Lácara. Directions: northeast on EX100 to La Roca de la Sierra, then east on local roads to La Nava de Santiago, then north to Cordobilla de Lácara. Continue east to the reservoir.

Embalse José Moreno, La Roca de la Sierra, day ticket (carp, tench). Fish from the first weekend in June to the last weekend in October. For tickets: Bar Pipo, C/Cardeña, Montijo. Directions: northeast on EX100 to La Roca de la Sierra.

Río Gevora, La Codosera, free fishing (trout, barbel, some black bass). Fast water with slower sections, a narrow river with abundant vegetation. The trout season goes from the middle of March. Directions: north EX110, just before Alburquerque go west on local roads towards La Codosera, passing the Ermita de Carrión. The road crosses the channel at Benavente and again leaving La Codosera heading north. Charcas de San Vicente, San Vicente de Alcántara, day ticket, various waters (tench, carp, mini-carp). Easy access: abundant fishing, clear water in attractive surroundings. Open from: June 1 to September 30. For tickets go to: Bar la Galleta, C/Juan Rodríguez, 6, San Vicente de Alcántara. Directions: north EX110/C530 to San Vicente.

Pantano de Alpotrel, San Vicente de Alcántara, day ticket (carp, black bass, barbel, tench, nase, mini-carp). Clear water with a rocky shoreline. It supplies San Vicente with drinking water so it's clean. Carp here to a good size. Fishing is off and on. Tickets from: José A Beltrán, Sociedad de Pesca la Tenca, Ayuntamiento, San Vicente. Directions: north EX110 to San Vicente de Alcántara.

Charco Frio, Río Guadiana, Medellín and Mengabril, day ticket (carp, barbel, black bass). Home to the barbel. Directions: east NV/E90 to Mérida, then northeast exit to Santa Amalia, and southeast to Medellín (birthplace of Hernán Cortés the conqueror of Mexico). Mengabril is south east.

Embalse de Orellana, Orellana la Vieja and Navalvillar de Pelá, free fishing (carp, pike, black bass, sunfish, crab). Some big carp to 30kg. Large pike and bass to 4kg. Nice surroundings with much wildlife, the water goes deep 20 to 50 metres. Many areas to fish:

1. At the tail-end of the reservoir. Good here for bass. This section is within 2km of the dam wall of the Embalse de García de Sola. The rest of the water is accessible from the highway that goes along the lake's left bank. Water levels vary with the seasons. It's ideal for carp as long as the level is stable.

2. Puente de Casas de Don Pedro. From the road from Casas de Don Pedro to Talarrubias. From this point the reservoir begins to gradually shallow out until the end.

3. Puente del Cogolludo, where it gets deeper. This is a good spot for carp, bass and pike up to the dam. Intermittent deep and shallow spots. Fishing is good. Access is ok via local roads, except along the Puente de Cogolludo itself. Carp weighing 20kg landed. The pike average 5kg and can be caught on spinners from the bank. The old road from Orellana to Puebla de Alcocer is a 14km bone-shaker, but it got anglers to virgin waters. A new road has opened this place up to all, so it's no longer that special, e.g. there is a litter problem and some noise at the weekends.

The Orellana reservoir's dam wall is near the Orellana town. On the opposite bank to the *presa*, in the Café Lola, take a look at the photos of big fish taken by local anglers. A 24-kilo carp was landed in 2002 at a spot about 5km up the lake from the dam, by the small yacht club. It was caught on a Spanish bean.
A drain, built from the Embalse de Zújar to the Embalse de Orellana to

prevent the latter drying up during times of drought, has resulted in the introduction from the former of lots of smaller fish. This is good news for the local match fishermen. Boats are permitted from the Puente de Cogolludo to the dam. Permission is obtainable from the Confederación Hidrográfica del Guadiana in Badajoz. Directions: east NV/E90 to Mérida, continuing east on A5, then N430 towards Ciudad Real, at Acedera exit south to Orellana la Vieja.

Coto de Puerto Peña, Río Guadiana, Talarrubias, day ticket, (pike, carp, common and royal). Set in wonderful countryside. *Tramo* (fishing stretch) length is 1.5 km. Big carp to 20kg and big pike. Fish from the Presa de García Sola to the confluence of the San Román stream with the Río Guadiana, on its left bank. For tickets: Bar El Poblado, Puerto Peña. Where to stay? Talarrubias has a first-class campsite. Directions: east A5/E90 to Mérida, continuing east on A5, then N430 towards Ciudad Real, to Puerto Peña.

Spain's most important fishery and research centre, **Piscifactoría Las Vegas del Guadiana**, is based at Villafranco del Guadiana near Badajoz. This is a big operation. A good time to visit is between May and July when the highlight is the carp spawning (*freza*).

Operated by the Junta de Extremadura, the centre specialises in breeding programmes of fish species native to Extremadura, e.g barbel, Iberian nase, mini-carp and *calandinos* (a chub-like native species). Other regional native species found in their aquariums include *jarabugo* (Spanish minnow) and *fiaile* (Mummichog).

The centre also produces two million tench fry annually in 25 pools, 30 per cent of which go to the environmental authority (*Medio Ambiente*) and the rest to local fishing organisations. It maintains floating raft ponds for juvenile tench on the Embalse de Zújar. There are five adult tench ponds for improving the gene pool. Twenty ponds are dedicated to reproduction of common and royal carp.

Started in the late 1960s, the operation was significantly extended in 1988 with the opening of an educational interpretation centre, open to the public. Priorities are education, conservation and research into fish reproduction in the wild and in captivity.

Address: Centro de Acuicultura, Piscifactoría Las Vegas del Guadiana, Antigua Ctra. NV, km 391,7, 06195 Villafranco del Guadiana (Badajoz). Tel: 924 012 950. Email: rvelasco@aym.juntaex.es Or visit: www.juntaex.es/consejerias/aym/dgm/ays/acuicultura/centro.htm

Embalse de García de Sola, Valdecaballeros, free fishing (pike, black bass, carp, barbel, sun fish). Great landscape, abundant fishing. The borders are easy to get to and you can fish from a boat (permitted May 15-October 15). Inlets alternate with deeper areas of stony bottom. There are five popular spots. 1. Zona de la Isla. This zone, at La Barca de Peloche (ferry), is excellent for barbel. Before reaching Valdecaballeros take a dirt track for 6km. The zone is 1.5km before the bridge. Catch big carp from the bank here. Fishing for bass near the two bridges in the vicinity of Castilblanco is particularly good. 2. By the Valdecaballeros sluice (tail-end), good for carp and bass from April through May on surface decoys. Good accommodation here. Carry on up the same road. 3. Carp and barbel also good by the bridge near Herrera del Duque where the Río Guadalapejo enters the lake. 4. The best platform for fishing for barbel is below the dam by Puerto Peña. Bass and pike stocking terminated in 1985. 5. Zona de Peloche: from Herrera del Duque take minor road to Peloche and the dam. The margins have lots of submerged trees which provide a great angling environment for bass and pike. Catch them on Texas vinyls and Rapalas from 5-7cm. Fly also works well here. In Peloche there is a shallow, inclined beach.

Pike best in winter. A lot of tench. Try near Herrera del Duque. It can get tricky so be careful. Around Valdecaballeros, try at the Rivera del García, by the pharmacy and by the forge. Give it a go by the Bar de Machaca in front of the fishmonger's. Fish at the Laguna de los Leones. For tickets: Hogar de Pensionistas or the Bar La Fragua (apparently the landlord is very grumpy), Valdecaballeros. Directions: east E90 for Mérida, then east N430 past San Pedro, north to Valdecaballeros.

Embalse de Cijara, Río Guadiana, Herrera del Duque, free fishing (black bass, pike, carp, barbel, Iberian nase, pumpkinseed). This is on the eastern edge of Extremadura, bordering Toledo province. A pretty location, it's easy to spot fish here in the clear water. Built in 1956, the dam is 80 metres high and 295 metres long. A big reservoir with lots of difficult areas to fish. By boat you can go right around. This is a blessing since the lake is surrounded by private property. When the water level is high, the tail-ends are very good to fish from a craft. However, it can get busy with more than 30 boats on some days. The fishing isn't prolific, but there are some big 'uns out there. In Cijara livebaiting is allowed on up to three rods. The best times for pike are November to February. An 18kg pike was landed in April, 2003, on a Rapala plug. For bass (up to 2kg) visit March to May and September-October. There are few fish but they grow big. Fish for them using green worm lures in the zone of the viaducts (near Santa Quiteria) and the opposite bank by Helechosa de los Montes. On foot fish by the Bohonal, Estinilla and Puente Grande zones. The best places are by the dam, at El Chorrillo next to the viaduct and over by the football field. There are some carp. But it's best by boat for easy access to the inlets since you may need to walk a long way to find the best swims. Directions: east A5/E90, after Mérida branch east on N430, then north on EX316, continuing past Castilblanco on N502, then southeast to Helechosa and around the reservoir to Bohonal.

> The Fish are easy to spot in the clear waters of the Embalse de Cijara. It's a big reservoir with lots of difficult areas to fish. By boat you can go right around

Embalse La Serena, Talarrubias, free fishing (carp, barbel, black bass, pike, catfish). Built in 1990, this is the biggest reservoir in Spain and the third biggest in Europe. It averages 70 per cent capacity. The dam wall is 90 metres high with a hydro-electric power station. Connected to the Embalse de Orellana, 14 km below at the tail-end of the water. The fishing is best in spring. Vague accounts of pike here. Catfish have been caught in the Río Guadalmez shortly before the dam. There are many submerged trees by the shore, which creates a good habitat for bass.

Zone 1: driving west from Siruela towards Talarrubias, take a left towards Sancti-Spiritus, then almost immediately go right to a junction with a Stop sign. Access is over a cattle grid at the end of a 7km track. The shoreline has a backdrop of oak trees.

Zone 2: from Talarrubias take C413 northeast towards Herrera del Duque. Before reaching a white house turn right down the track, in good repair, to the lake. Pilgrims go this way every year to celebrate at the shrine of San José.

Zone 3: from Puebla de Alcocer drive towards Talarrubias and turn right towards Siruela. Head for the bridge over the reservoir but don't cross. Facing the shore, go right down the old road to the bank. Leave your car at the entrance and foot it. The banks either side of the bridge are ok. Once you cross over, find the old road on the left that takes you to the tail-end of the water. It looks promising here.

Directions: east A5/E90 to Mérida, continue east on A5, then take N430, turn right southeast to Talarrubias.

Santiaguito, Río Zújar, Villanueva de la Serena, day ticket (carp, black bass). This stretch of the Zújar is near a big town so the water level will vary greatly. However, the fishing is fine. For tickets: Bar Turismo, C/Hernán Cortés, 225, Villanueva. Directions: east A5/E90 for Mérida, then east A5, then N430 for Villanueva de la Serena. Take local roads east of town for the channel.

Embalse de El Paredón, Campanario, day ticket, (carp, tench). Carp here are ok. The water is cloudy. For tickets: Bar los Cristales, C/Real, 2, Campanario. Directions: east NV/E90 to Mérida, then east again NV/N430, south to Villanueva de la Serena and southeast on EX104 to Campanario.

Hornachos, Los Molinos, Ribera de Fresno and Hinojosa del Valle (black bass, carp, barbel). Very pretty place — spot the herons at dusk. There is good access from the road to the bank. Many spots for bass in the inlets and promontories. Look out for deeper holes. In summer there is a litter problem by the dam, so try the zone of Minbero, really beautiful. Directions: to Mérida, then south on A66 Zafra-Seville road. At Villafranco de los Barros, take a left on EX342 for Ribera, Hornachos and the lake.

Presa de Nogales, Nogales, free fishing (carp, tench, mini-carp, barbel). A nice setting, the small cork oak trees feed the local pigs but don't offer enough shade to the angler in summer when the shoreline recedes. This is made up for by the great views. Directions: from Badajoz N432 to Santa Marta, then west to Nogales. The reservoir is just to the south.

Embalse de Piedra Aguda, Río Olivenza, Badajoz, day ticket (carp, barbel, black bass, nase, tench, *pardilla* {mini-carp}). Pretty water with lots of bass. For tickets: Bar El Rincón at Olivenza. Also try the Sociedad de Cazadores and Pexadores La Oliventina. Directions: south EX107 to

Olivenza, then east EX105 towards Valverde.

Olivenza, various waters, free fishing (carp, barbel, tench). A lot of smaller fish caught around here. Try the canal near Villarreal (a lot of big barbel and some nice-size carp) and Puente Ajuda — the locals use bird seed (*cañamon*) to catch barbel here in the current. Directions: south EX107 to Olivenza.

Embalse de Cuncos, Villanueva del Fresno, day ticket (carp). For tickets: Bar el Pilar and Bar la Esquina, Villanueva. Directions: south EX107 to Villanueva del Fresno.

Embalse Zaos, Oliva de la Frontera and Jerez de los Caballeros, *pesca sin muerte* (carp, barbel, tench, sunfish). Good fishing in a small shallow lake with a nice setting. Access is difficult. Fish from the foot of Santuario de la Virgen de Gracia. The dam is located 2km from Oliva de la Frontera via a single track. Access is easier coming from the other direction to the opposite bank. There is a snack bar at the back of the water alongside the local canoeing club. Lots of big carp here. Directions: south N432/N435 to Jerez, then west EX112 to Oliva. Charca La Albuera, Jerez de los Caballeros, free fishing and day ticket (tench). Open first weekend of June to the first weekend of September. For tickets: Deportes Gordillo in Jerez. Directions: south N432/N435 to Jerez.

Embalse de Valuengo, Jerez de los Caballeros, day ticket (common and royal carp, barbel, tench, black bass). One of the province's better waters, 150 hectares in area. This is a pretty spot with lots of wildfowl. The shoreline was cleaned in 2002. Good-size carp, lots of barbel. The winning weight in 2002 for a provincial championship was 22kg. The dam, 33 metres high and 197 metres long, was built in 1958. It is supplied by the Río Ardila.

Royal carp were introduced in 1969. In 1989 tench were caught for the first time. There are fewer fish than before but average bag weights have increased. Fish before the dam by the second grill. The shortest access route is via Jerez. Good access to all the fishing platforms on the left bank. Leave your car on the adjacent unfinished road — there is plenty of space — and foot it to the bank. For tickets: Bar Sebastián in Valuengo, tel: 924 730 173; Bar Azul in Jerez, tel: 924 730 823; Bar Pepe in Brovales, tel: 924 731 615; Deportes Gordillo, Barricada de Pumar s/n, tel: 924 750 162. Directions: south N432/N435 to Jerez, then to Valuengo and east.

Embalse de Burguillos, Charco El Toro, day ticket (tench). Open from May 15 to the last weekend in September. Not open on holidays. For tickets: Bar El Francés, Avda. de la Constitución,1, Burguillos. Directions: southeast N432 to Zafra then west N435 and side road to Burguillos. Embalse de los Valles, Los Valles, Valle de Matamoros, day ticket (tench). Open from May 15 to September 30. Not open on holidays. For tickets: Bar El Tumba, Valle de Santa Ana, tel: 924 753 712; Bar El Nene, Valle de Matamoros. Directions: south N432/N435 to Valle de Matamoros, just before Jerez de los Caballeros.

Embalse de Albuera de Castellar, Albuera, free fishing and day ticket (carp, barbel, mini-carp, black bass, sun fish). Ten per cent of the water is accessible by car via the dam. This is a medium-sized water with a lot of big carp and barbel and the occasional bass. In summer the level gets low. Take a brolly – there is no shade. For tickets: Bar los Pescadores, Zafra, tel: 924 550 755; Pesca los Cipris Zafra, tel: 924 553 001. Directions: southeast N432 to Zafra then local roads southwest to Alconera.

↓ Cáceres

Cáceres is an exceptionally beautiful place. To the west is the old town of Alcántara, close to the Portuguese border, with an impressive Roman bridge spanning the Río Tajo. Try a bottle of Fuente Vieja rosé wine (*vino rosado*) from Villafranco de los Barros. On Saturday mornings tune into Linde y Ribera, a well-known angling show on Onda Cero radio, hosted by Cesáreo Martín. It goes out between 7 and 8am. Email him at lindeyribera@ondacero.es. He will read out on air news of any big catches by visiting anglers – celebrity awaits you.

In September 2003 local angling interests and the Cáceres city council jointly spent 300,000 euros to regenerate the rundown angling pools on the town's Charca Musia industrial estate. Altogether 12,000 tench were added to the 200 kilos of existing stock fish, six fishing platforms were installed, and an angling school established.

Licences: Servicio Territorial de la Consejería de Obras Públicas, Urbanismo y Medio Ambiente, C/García Plata de Osma, 1, Cáceres. Tel: 927 001 000.

Angling information: Juan Romero Hernández, Federación Extremeña de Pesca, C/Chantre, 3 Bajo, Plasencia. PO Box: Apartado de Correos 463, 10600 Plasencia. Tel/fax: 927 424 955. www.interbook.net/personal/fedextpesca. Permission to fish the *cotos* (fishing reserves) can be obtained from this federation and Medio Ambiente.

Boat licences: Confederación Hidrográfica del Tajo, Edificio de Servicios Múltiples Gral, Primo de Rivera, 2-6a, 10001 Cáceres. Tel: 927 221 900. Fax: 927 225 651.

Meet fellow anglers at Club Bassextremedura, C/José Martínez Ruiz "Azorín", Edif. Zeus, Portal 2-2A, 06800 Mérida. Tel: 670 883 825. Email: bassextremedura@bassextremedura.com

Directions are given for a start at Cáceres.

Coto de Sierra Brava, Río Pizarroso, Zorita and Madrigalejo, day ticket (pike, black bass, carp, sun fish). A very popular local spot in a pretty location. The water is clear and clean. Loads of bass and lots of pike. Use spinners to catch them. Catches of 13kg and 16kg reported in the tail-end of the water. Enter this zone via Zogrosan at the sugar factory. Best in spring for the largest bass. Good at all other times. For tickets: Bar El Cazador, Madrigalejo. Directions: east N521 to Trujillo, then south EX208 passing Zorita, south on EX355 towards Madrigalejo.

Embalse de Sierra Brava, Madrigalejo, free fishing (pike, black bass). Clear water. It goes from three to 25 metres in depth. This is a popular water. Bass caught to 3kg and pike to 12.5kg. Just remember that the pumpkinseed will go straight for your worm jigglers. Directions: east N521 to Trujillo, then south EX208 passing Zorita, south on EX355 towards Madrigalejo.

Various waters of **Carrizosa**, Madrigalejo, free with special regulations (carp, trout). Fish for trout only in season with a day ticket. Closed on holidays. For tickets: la Sociedad El Cachuelo. Directions: as for the Sierra Brava reservoir.

Embalse de Valdesalor, Cáceres, day ticket (carp, barbel, black bass). Bass are aloof but large. This is a pretty family spot, marred by a litter problem at weekends. For tickets, try the Valdesalor bars. Directions: south on N630, exit east at Valdesalor towards Torreorgaz.

Embalse de Guadiloba, Cáceres, day ticket (carp, tench). A few barbel. Catfish have made an appearance recently. A popular spot for Spanish fishermen. This is also a place to bring the family for a fish. There are loads of small carp. A 20kg bag in a morning is commonplace. Directions: east on N521 for about 7km then north on minor road.

Río Almonte, Monroy, day ticket (black bass, royal and common carp, common barbel). A smallish river with lots of barbel that will take a dry fly. They go like the clappers on light tackle. Park near the bridge on the Trujillo highway. Walk along the river bank to find the best spot. Quite popular at the weekends with local anglers and the accessible area is quite restricted. For tickets: Bar de La Fábrica at Monroy. Directions: north-northeast on EX390 towards Monroy.

Río Ibor, Mesas and Bohonal de Ibor, free fishing, (barbel). Big barbel that fight hard. Catch them on worm or nymph-type flies. This is a typical river of the local mountains. It is very narrow and not an easy place to cast because of the trees. The fishing itself is easy. From April the barbel run up the river when the water level is sufficient. Try worm or maggots. The downstream zone is more popular. Fish by the old mill. The main access is by the Puente de Mesas.

Directions: east N521 to Trujillo, then north A5 to Almaraz, now east on local roads to Bohonal de Ibor. From Madrid, take the A5 towards Cáceres. Exit south near Navalmoral de la Mata for Peraleda de la Mata. Continue to Bohonal de Ibor. Just past the traffic lights and speeding sign a road leads right to Mesas de Ibor. Between Bohonal and Mesas de Ibor look for an entrance before a bridge over the channel. Leave the car here and fish the river, if it's up. If not, return to the highway, cross to the right of the bridge. A footpath runs along the channel to the right of the river.

Embalse de Almaraz, Río Tajo, Almeraz and Saucidilla, free fishing (carp, black bass). This is one of the best places to catch bass in the depth of winter. It has an industrial backdrop. The adjacent nuclear power station heats this reservoir's water. Even in freezing conditions the water can reach 20 degrees C in places. Creating many thermal layers, it provides the right conditions for bass fishing. However the vegetation is dense and bullrushes cover the banks. Even so, it's possible in a few places to cast from the bank and it's as good as from a boat. The locals can use waders because it is shallow at the margins (one metre deep). Zone 1. Highest part of the reservoir. Access is via the road between Almaraz, just north, and Saucedilla, which goes over the dam. 2. Right bank from dam to the power station. The water here is cooler but the bass grow bigger. Take a track west from Almaraz. 3. From the dam car park, take the left bank, following it for 2km around until it reaches the power station perimeter fence. This is a good spot for bass. Directions: east N521 to Trujillo, then north A5 to Almaraz.

Embalses de Torrejón-Tajo, Torrejón-Tiétar and Alcántara, Alcántara, Coria and Acehuche, day ticket and free fishing (carp, black bass, barbel, comizo and common). Fish for free from the dam walls of the Torrejón-Tajo and Torrejón-Tiétar reservoirs to the new bridge (*puente nuevo*) at Villarreal de San Carlos. As many as 50 bass averaging 1kg have been caught by one angler in a day. The level varies greatly as the floodgates of the Torrejón dam, upstream, are opened regularly. For tickets and information on where to fish for free, visit Villarreal. Near the Alcántara reservoir, visit the Bar Fori in Acehuche for day tickets and free fishing information. Directions: for Torrejón-Tajo, from Cáceres take country road EX390 northeast to Torrejón el Rubio, then north on EX208 to the Villarreal bridge. To approach the Embalse de Alcántara, go north N630, which runs alongside reservoir. To reach Acehuche, continue north on EX109 towards Coria, turning east on EX372.

Fishing Extremadura

Julian Hunter, from Inverness, shares some of his angling experiences in Extremadura, particularly the area around Cáceres:

"Most of my trips to Spain have been spent cycling with a telescopic rod attached to my crossbar and not much equipment or bait. This can prove a good way to fish as you can leave your bike behind a bush when you spot a good swim and nobody knows you are there. However, in 2004 we hired a car and took more paraphernalia with us. The more tackle I take the less fish I catch. I recommend using 1:200,000 provincial maps, available from Stanfords in Covent Garden, London.

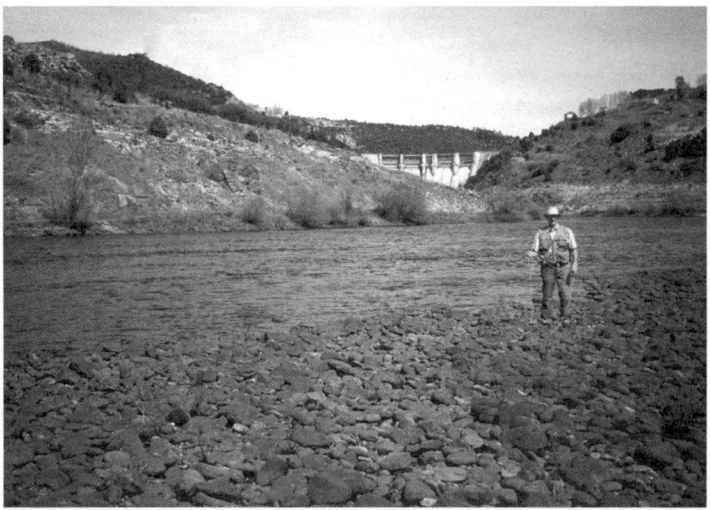

PHOTO COURTESY OF JULIAN HUNTER

Julian Hunter's friend Richard at Dos Ríos at the confluence of the Tormes and Duero rivers with the huge dam in the background

The whole of the Río Tajo is artificially controlled with reservoirs, from the Portuguese border all the way to Monfragüe and most of the way up to Talavera de la Reina.

We started at the Monfragüe natural park just to the northeast of Cáceres. There is a very useful centre, with accommodation at the Posada El Arriero, in the village of Torrejón el Rubio. The Ayuntamiento (town hall) will sell you tickets for several small reservoirs. One, the Embalse de Jarrallana, is roughly 3km from the village on the Cáceres road, then a left turn. It is very pretty, but we didn't catch many fish. The Embalse de La Vid, east of the village, is highly regarded by local anglers.

We next fished just to the north, at the Embalses de Torrejón-Tajo and Torrejón-Tiétar within the park, but they are rocky and proved an uncomfortable angling experience. Day tickets can be purchased in the park office at Villarreal de San Carlos.

Further west from Torrejón el Rubio on the Cáceres road, we fished the Río Almonte near Monroy and caught several small common barbel

→

→ "(barbo común) but it is quite popular at weekends and the fishable area is limited. We bought tickets in the Bar de la Fábrica at Monroy. The next day we headed west past Cáceres. A good centre to stay is the Hotel El Ciervo at Aliseda on the road from Cáceres to Alcántara. Nearby is the pretty Río Salor. From our hotel we drove down the Alcántara road and took the first right turn which soon crosses the river. A few metres upstream of the bridge there is a lovely lake which seems to have black bass — one went for my spinner. A wildlife guide there told me that the best centre for tench ponds is at Malpartida de Cáceres, but we did not have time to fish any of them.

The huge Embalse de Alcántara offers free fishing, but it is very bare. A boat would be a good idea. There may be fishing in the Río Tajo immediately below the huge dam at Alcántara, above and below the Puente Romano. There is no access road to the river downstream of Alcántara, but it might be worth going all the way down to Cedillo on the border with Portugal, which is the next road access. The whole river channel between these two towns forms the Embalse de Cedillo. Further around is the Río Alagón, to the north of the Embalse de Alcántara at Coria. Tickets for the water can be purchased at the bus station snack bar. The best swims are well downstream of the town as the river channel enters a steep gorge where there is a ruined weir and mill. I caught one barbo comizo at this spot. It is quite popular with locals.

The Embalse de Gabriel y Galán, to the north of Plasencia, looks good. We cycled past it and the locals were catching carp with a weighted treble hook! There is good accommodation at the Hostal Jacinto in Zarza de Granadilla. I have had some great times fishing with my friends in Extremadura — although not always with huge catches.'

Embalse de Valdeobispo, Valdeobispo, free fishing (pike, sun fish, barbel, carp, black bass). Loads of barbel. This is a clear-water reservoir used for irrigation. The depth varies greatly because of the uneven bottom. The locals say this is the most beautiful dam in all of Spain. Lots of birds such as Egyptian vultures. There is a bathing zone by the dam. The water is surrounded by private property, which can make access problematical away from the main access roads. Directions: north N630 to Plasencia, then EX370 west, then northwest to Valdeobispo.

Río Alagón, Coria, free fishing, (carp, common barbel and comizo barbel). Clear water with deep pools in places, stony bottom in others, usually a full water level. The locals complain there are too many carp. It's easy here to catch barbel and bass to a very good size. Directions: from Cáceres go north on N630, then EX109. Just before Coria there is a bridge over the river Alagón. Access from Coria centre to the riverbank is easy.

Embalse del Prado de la Monja, Acebo, free fishing (trout, barbel). Clear water and lots of fish. Quite deep. Beautiful setting and peaceful. Directions: go north on N630, then EX109. Pass Coria and Moraleja, heading towards Ciudad Rodrigo. Exit west towards Acebo. The lake is located 5km away from Acebo.

Río Salor, Herreruela, Membrío, free fishing (pike, black bass, carp, barbel). A nice setting. March to September is the best time to visit. This is a fast water in winter with high levels, becoming wide channels in summer with little depth. Therefore floating baits and lures are recommended. Directions: west N521 past Herreruela then Salorino. The road bridge crosses the channel.

Embalse Molano, Arroyo de La Luz, day ticket (carp, barbel). Clear water with easy access to the reservoir. It is surrounded by a wire fence to stop the cattle degrading the bank. Catch bass to 1kg on light tackle and try fishing with a fly or a spinner. Fish at the margins for bass in their natural habitat of submerged trees with a surface lure. But be prepared to alter your tactics when the water level changes. The nice carp fall to fly here as well. For tickets: Casa de la Cultura, Arroyo. Directions: west N521, then northwest EX207 to Arroyo.

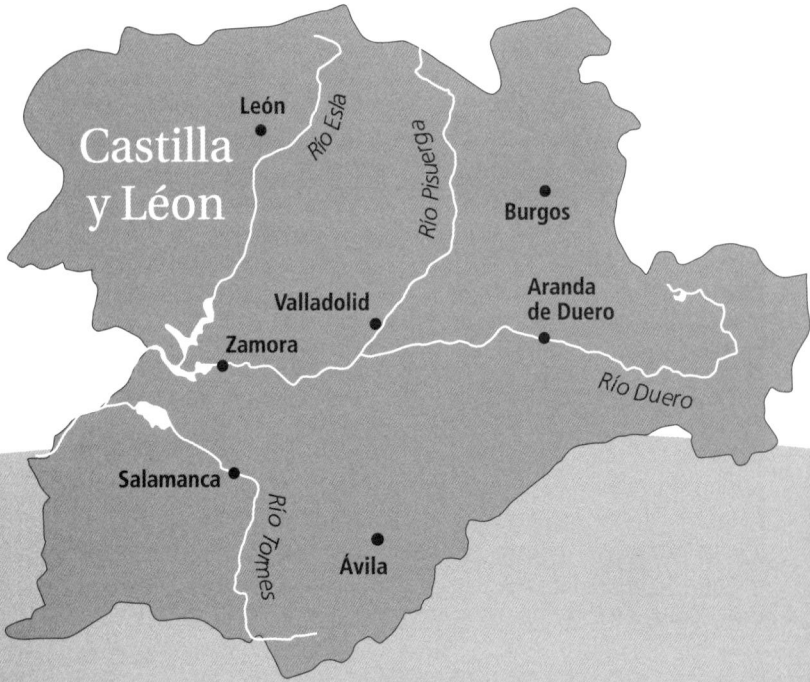

Castilla
y Léon

León

Río Esla

Río Pisuerga

Burgos

Valladolid

Aranda
de Duero

Zamora

Río Duero

Salamanca

Río Tormes

Ávila

Castilla y Léon

CHAPTER SEVEN

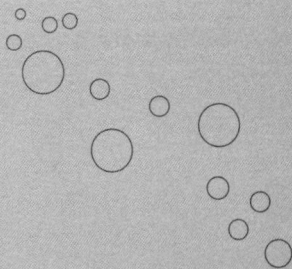

↓ Castilla y León

Northern Spain's angling reputation rests squarely on the lovely trout rivers around León (lying in the region known as Castilla y León). Some are included in this chapter, but will be treated more fully in Santana's book on game fishing. So what about the coarse fishing scene? Angling locations surround Valladolid, Ávila, Burgos, León, Salamanca and Zamora.

The main river, the Duero, flows from east to west passing Valladolid and Zamora and entering Portugal to exit at Oporto on the Atlantic coastline. Absence of heavy industry on the Spanish section makes this area one of the cleanest regions in the peninsula. This is good news for anglers.

> This region offers technically the most diverse range of challenges to the visiting angler. It's reputation rests squarely on the lovely trout rivers around Léon

To the west of Zamora, where the Duero has been dammed for a series of reservoirs, it flows through deep rocky gorges with difficult access. It is easiest to fish here around bridges or dams. Further north and to the east, the rivers flow through flatter agricultural land and access proves much easier around Benavente (Río Esla) and Toro (Río Duero).

The Castilla y León region offers technically the most diverse range of challenges to the visiting angler. To catch barbel in small, fast-flowing upland streams such as the Aliste and Tera requires a mobile approach. Zander have made it to the upper Ebro — will you? The eels at Carucedo grow bigger than the tench and trout that inhabit the mountain reservoir at Barcena. But not as big as the carp of Almendra, or the pike in the Esla and Orbigo rivers.

It makes perfect sense to combine your coarse angling holiday with trips to the great cathedral cities of León, Burgos and Salamanca. Remember that this region, though hot enough in summer, is a better bet for a visit at that time than inland Andalusia, which turns into a frying pan during July and August.

How about angling licences? See the information for the different provinces.

Information: Federación Castellano-Leonesa de Pesca, Avda. Ramón Praderas, s/n (Feria de Muestras), 47009 Valladolid. Tel: 983 429 303. www.fedpescacyl.com; also at Avda. José Antonio, 125, 24001 León. Tel: 987 655 312, 987 655 312. Fax: 987 655 312.

Boat licences (there are offices in all the main cities): Confederación Hidrográfica del Duero, Comisaría de Aguas, C/Muro, 5, 47004 Valladolid. Tel: 983 215 400. Fax: 983 215 438. Email: mbl@chduero.es. www.chduero.es

Accommodation: visit: www.salamancaturismo.com/agua.htm or email: reservas@salamancaturismo.com Tel: 902 170 623 (Ciudad Rodrigo). The site offers hotel rooms and tourist activities for the whole of the Salamanca region. And provides some nice photography, suggesting new places you may like to fish and enjoy.

⬇ Burgos

All directions are given for a start at Burgos.

Licences: S.T.M.A., C/Juan de Padilla, s/n, 09071 Burgos.Tel: 947 281 558, 947 281 404. Fax: 947 237 959. Email: Licencias.cazaypesca. bu@jcyl.es

Embalse de Sobrón, Miranda del Ebro, Río Ebro system, free fishing (carp, barbel, black bass). The nuclear power station at Garona creates warm thermals. The reservoir is shared with Álava, however their section has difficult access. There are catfish near the dam. Zander get a mention. *Perca sol* (pumpkinseed or sun fish) are on the up. Directions: N1 or E5 northeast for Miranda, near Pancorbo exit north on BU525, exit west for Sobrón.

Río Ebro, Valdivieso, Manzanedo, free fishing (trout, barbel, carp). Nice scenery. The prettiest and most difficult spot to access is Los Hocinos, which has a very rocky middle channel, with strong current and calmer eddies with deep holes. Sediment in the water gives it a colour typical for the Ebro. When it rains, the water becomes opaque. 15-20 metres wide. Popular with local anglers. Directions: north N623 then CL629 for Valdenoceda, then to Incinillas and Manzanedo. The road follows the channel so it's easy.

↓ Ávila

Licences: Servicio Territorial de Medio Ambiente, Pza Santa Ana, s/n, 05071 Ávila. Tel: 920 355 171. Fax: 920 353 067. Email: Licencias. cazaypesca.av@jcyl.es

Embalse de Voltoya, Coto de Voltoya, Ávila (carp, tench, catfish, trout, barbel). Easy access but water level may drop low in summer. Fish to left of the dam. Directions: from Ávila go east 25km on N110, turn south for the reservoir.

↓ León

Licences: S.T.M.A., Avda. Peregrinos, s/n, 24071 León. Tel: 987 296 159/189. Fax: 987 296 125. Email: Licencias.cazaypesca.le@jcyl.es
Fly fishing shop: Antuñez, José Antonio, 25, 24001 León. Tel: 987 220 266/449 216.

All directions are given for a start at León.

Embalse de Barcena, Barcena, free fishing (carp, black bass, trout). Boats allowed. This is a mountain reservoir with clean, clear water and a reputation for rod-breaking fish. It can be spotted 40km away on the A6 road; twin plumes of steam rise from the adjacent cooling towers.

View of Embalse de Barcena looking north (near Ponferrada)

Too steep to fish at the dam, where the Confederación Hidrográfica building is located. They can advise on best places to fish.

It is good for tench. Recently the bass have come good, reaching 2kg caught weight. Not many trout except in the tail and where the Río Boeza enters. This is not a listed trout *coto*, so you can catch trout at this water with just the standard regional angling licence. The maximum bass kill limit is reduced to five fish. A lot of small royals and some commons. Locals say the lake is not as good as it was. There are a lot of Iberian nase in the central section. Late in season, when the drop in water level will make access problematic for the whole reservoir, you can attempt access at the private boat club on the east shore, with permission.

Directions: west N120/A6 for 60km. From Ponferrada take the N631 that goes north to Toreno. Now follow the signs for the power station, go past it and through a small narrow tunnel on to recreational areas by the shoreline.

Lago de Carucedo, Barco de Valdeorras (black bass, nase, eels, carp). Clean water, pretty surroundings, one of Spain's few natural lakes. And a more manageable alternative if the sheer scale of the Barcena reservoir proves intimidating. The site is split into three waters. The

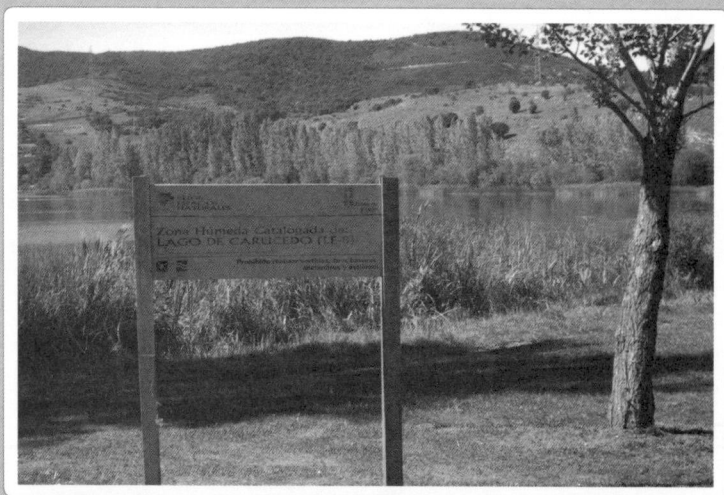

Lago de Carucedo located west of Ponferrada

bottom lake has the best access. It is 400 metres from town and has a lovely beach swim. The next lake up has the biggest carp. The eels are enormous. Bass are down – some say Embalse de Peñarrubia, 6km away, is better. Access to a few areas is good, otherwise problematic.

Directions: southwest from Ponferrada on the N536. At Carucedo turn right at Mesón El Lago then 400 metres down a good dirt track to the bottom lake. Access to the middle lake: just before the dam, take left turn down to bottom and follow track around to lake. Best swim is opposite concrete outhouse. Cast to the far bank where a point divides inlet from main area of water. Three more swims adjacent. Accommodation: Mesón El Lago, Ctra N536, 24442 Carucedo, Tel: 987 422 846. On the evening menu are the eels they catch in the lake.

The distinctive landscape around Carucedo was created by the Romans who mined vast quantities of gold. Established tracks provide a distracting afternoon walk around the site for bored anglers. Roman strip-mining activities blocked the valley to form three lakes.

More romantically, it is said that a mermaid called Xama Cariseda was scorned by a Carucedo man and her tears filled the valley, drowning all the inhabitants. The lakes formed as the waters receded. Las Médulas, 3km up the valley from Carucedo, is a tourist centre with many restaurants and pensions.

Villimer, free fishing (trout). Directions: take N601 towards Valladolid to Villarente. Turn off east for Villafañé, then north to Villimer for the Piscifactoría (trout farm).

Río Orbigo, Cebrones del Río, free fishing (pike, barbel). The river channel is fishable for a 15km stretch between Bañeza and Benavente. Fish for the big pike upstream of Cebrones where the water is held back. Use poppers or crayfish fly imitations. It can get weedy, so give the big S a go as well. Bañeza is good for accommodation and restaurants. Directions: CL622 south west from León 40 km to Bañeza/Benavente.

↓ Zamora

Never conquered by the Moors, the fish as a symbol of early Christianity is evident in the architecture of the Byzantine cathedral at Zamora. It is covered in glorious fishtail patterns (see page 7). There is a tackle shop, San Lázaro, on Avenida da Galicia, in Zamora.

All directions are given for a start at Zamora.

Licences: Servicio Territorial de Medio Ambiente, C/Leopolda Alas Clarín, 4, 49071 Zamora. Tel: 980 559 600/980 510 361. Fax: 980 526 991. Email: Licencias.cazaypesca.za@jcyl.es

Arroyo Ahogaborricos, Río Orbigo, Benavente, free fishing (tench, carp, black bass, pike). Calm water, one metre deep, weed in summer. Directions: north N630 to Benavente then northwest A6 to Pobladura del Valle.

Río Duero, Zamora, free fishing (carp, black bass, pike). The usual litter problems associated with urban environments, but not too bad. Fish the bank at Izda for comfort. There is easy access to most swims. Ledger to the deep holes. Good in May, June, July, August, when it is best at dawn or dusk. The Zona de Extremadura is good for bass and pike. Directions: throughout Zamora but best just upstream from city centre. Locate a canal off the main channel, adjacent to flats, a car park and the river jetty. This canal swim is two metres deep and full of tench and carp to 5kg that are caught on worm and sweetcorn. This swim is a favourite hotspot with local anglers.

Embalse de Castro de Alcañices, Castro de Alcañices, Río Duero system, free fishing (carp, barbel, trout, pike). Directions: take N122 northwest towards Alcañices. Near Fonfría turn off for Castro de Alcañices, then head for Salto de Castro.

Embalse de Ricobayo, Manzanal del Barco and Montamarta, free fishing (carp, barbel, pike, black bass). Clear deep waters with great rocky gorges, alternating with shallow, sloping banks. Take a lot of water with you to drink; in summer there is a lack of shade. Best spot for pike is by the dam. No livebaiting permitted, but you can eat the pike. The fine for livebaiting is 300 euros. In times of bad drought, this reservoir may be dry. Directions: N112 from Zamora to Ricobayo.

Pike fishing is an under-rated pastime in Spain. Given the abundance of carp and barbel, this may seem understandable. Its neglect seems less appropriate when one considers the excellent sport that can be easily accessed in most regions. The national record stands at 21.45kg, caught on the lower Río Esla near León. An old Spanish wives' tale claims that if you leave a pike's head on the doorstep your house will be safe from lightning strike.

Río Aliste, Gallegos del Río, free fishing (carp). Maximum depth is two metres. Water goes cloudy in summer, but is clear in winter. The Río Aliste ends at the Pantano de Ricobayo. This is exciting small-river fishing and the surroundings make the hike worthwhile. Directions: N112 from Zamora to Ricobayo. Northwest local roads 20km past Embalse de Ricobayo to towns along the river.

Río Esla, Benavente, free fishing (pike, trout *cotos* along route). Once a nationally renowned location for pike, this has declined slightly in recent years due to changes in water management. But it's still a top pike venue. Variable depth, tree-lined banks. Lots of big pike in winter. At Castropepe turn off the N630 at an orange bus shelter, keep to the right driving through the village down to a graveyard and river gauging station where fishing is possible. Upstream follow a big concrete drain through the village of Castrogonzalo, to the river where there is a pleasant park. Fish on the stone platforms between the trees. Further to the south, try at Bretocino where fishing is permitted upstream of the road bridge or downstream of the football field and the mill. The river is fished quite hard by Spanish standards. Some big barbel on the faster sections. Pike fall to fly. Try by the confluence with the Río Obrigo. Try at Las Salinas de Villafalila, where there is lots of wildfowl. In April it can flood and gets very silty. Directions: Zamora to Benavente. Just to southwest is Castrogonzalo near N630 and N630 junction.

Río Obrigo, free fishing, (pike, barbel, trout *cotos* on route). Río Obrigo has less fishing pressure than Río Esla. Fish for pike around Vecilla de la Polvorosa and Fresno de la Polvorosa. Pike to 12kg at the confluence of the three rivers, Obrigo, Tera, Esla). In summer fish at Santa Cristina by the bridge where you catch the school bus. Directions: just north of Benavente to the west of A6 main road.

Fly-fisherman on Río Orbigo west of Benavente, under the bridge on the N-525 road, facing upstream

Río Tera, Micereces de Tera, free fishing (barbel, black bass, pike, day tickets for trout fishing available on site). Two spots, from Las Quirulas, perfect for pike in shallow runs, and up to the Micereces bridge. There is easy access here. Catch barbel to a good size the other side. Directions: N630 to Benavente then west on N525 to Micereces.
Río Tera, Mozar de Valverde. A pretty, popular weekend picnic area, 20 minutes' drive southwest of Benavente situated right on the Río Tera. And a good place to start your kids fishing. I have witnessed a small boy catch five trout in one hour by trotting a float and sweetcorn by the road bridge. Day tickets for this stretch can be obtained from the bar across the road from the camping, except on Sunday. Trout fishing permitted from March 15 to October 31. Fifteen minutes' drive south of Valverde on the same road there are some pleasant, deeper stretches, accessible from a track from the village of Burganes de Valverde down to the riverside football field and picnic area. Camping Río Tera is handily situated next to the river.

⬇ Salamanca

Salamanca's main square, the Plaza Mayor, is the most splendid in all of Spain. The city is on the very select World Heritage list of sites. And you can even fish for barbel in the Río Tormes near the Roman bridge close to the city centre.

Licences: Servico Territorial de Medio Ambiente, C/Villar y Macías, 1a Planta, 37071 Salamanca. Tel: 923 296 049. Fax: 923 296 041. Email: Licencias.cazaypesca.sa@jcyl.es

Accommodation: Camping and cabins are available at the Hotel Regio 2km southeast of the city centre.

Embalse de Almendra, free fishing (carp, black bass, barbel, pike). You drive along the Tormes, one of the most beautiful rivers in Spain, en route to the reservoir. For trout, you need a day permit. There is superb pike and barbel sport in a glorious spot by the bridge at Baños de Ledesma. The embalse itself is a huge expanse of water, even when half-empty in September and October. The dam and causeway are 2km long. Rocky and sandy areas with some steep gorges and deep water. Many big carp and large pike easily in excess of 20kg.

When level is down, the exposed, lunar-like shoreline forms a hard surface to drive over to the right swims. If it is hard, turn right after causeway, north end at small hut or house and weave through gaps in maze of exposed old stone walls to left of inlet then back around to the right towards the main shoreline. Walk the last 600 metres to bank. Sometimes there are other anglers' car tracks to follow. If in doubt, ask at the campsite bar. The carp here respond well to sweetcorn after groundbaiting. The bites are very positive. Another spot, if you are brave enough, is to drive on the top of the causeway back towards the dam (but not at night) and fish into the wind to the left of the twin concrete jetties.

Fishing at Monleras is a good alternative. Drive through the village to the signposted track then 1km on to the shoreline.

Accommodation: Camping Los Arribes is located 2km north of the dam. Directions: Drive northwest from Salamanca on SA300 to Ledesma, then on SA302 to Almendra. From Almendra SA315 crosses the dam.

Down stream from the Almendra dam the Tormes flows into the Río Duero. Most of the water is piped to the Almendra power station, leaving only a small flow in the river. There are good bases at Fermoselle (Hotel de Liseda) on the CL527. At Villarino a narrow road leads down to Ambas Aguas (both waters) near the confluence of the waters. Here the Duero's level fluctuates rapidly due to the power station upstream, making it a difficult place to fish. Locals fish at the weekend when they say more stable conditions exist. The fish are mostly black bass, barbel and Iberian nase.

⬇ Valladolid

All directions are given for a start at Valladolid.

Licences (€8): Delegación Territorial, C/Duque de la Victoria, 5, 47001 Valladolid. Tel: 983 411 079/983 414 463. Fax: 983 411 090. Email: Licencias.cazaypesca.va@jcyl.es Open Friday-Saturday 9am-2pm, Monday-Thursday 9am-2pm and 4-6pm. Use the underground car park at Plaza de España. It's a 10-minute walk to the Junta office where they will issue you with a voucher. Cash this for your licence at the Caja España opposite the underground car park.

Tordesillas is a good central location to base your angling holiday. It is 40 minutes from Valladolid airport and right on the Río Duero – you can

Río Duero by the bridge at Tordesillas

Weir pool swim at Pesqueruela on the Río Duero near Simancas

start fishing right away at the beach bar by the bridge. Cabins can be hired at Camping El Astral just over the bridge.

Embalse de la Santa Espina, Coto de Santa Espina, Río Bajoz (carp). Only a few fishing spots, but a good place for tench, average weight half a kilo, which can be caught on the bottom using worms during the summer. Some go to 3kg. Try at the tail end. April to August is best. But watch out for the mosquitos. Directions: northwest from Valladolid on VA514 to Wamba, continue on VP5501 past Peñaflor de Hornija to Santa Espina monastery and Río Bajoz.

Canal de Castilla, Valladolid, free fishing (pike, sun fish, black bass). Pike over 10kg. The local villagers are said to get hot tempered with visiting anglers. Directions: any spot along the Valladolid-Palencia main road.

Pesqueruela, Río Duero, Valladolid, free fishing (barbel, carp, black bass, Iberian nase, sun fish). Clean water with many pools to fish due to the nature of the current. Depth runs two to three metres. Very popular with the local anglers from Valladolid. Two zones to fish, La Pesqueruela and the beach zone.

THE ESSENTIAL GUIDE TO COARSE FISHING IN SPAIN

La Pesqueruela (fishery) is a pond with a two-metre high weir, where the Río Pisuerga meets the Río Duero. Reported to be the best stretch on the Duero. It's one metre deep. You will require waders but it is very good here for smaller barbel. Local anglers catch 1kg barbel on a float rig that they bait up by simply dragging the hook against the weed on the weir by their feet and casting out into the torrent. A dozen barbel in a morning to 1kg is not exceptional for them.

In the beach zone, there are more pumpkinseed and nase. The carp average 2kg. The barbel average 0.75kg. Barbel are caught here to one metre in length out in the main channel. This is 10 to15 metres straight out when casting left at 90 degrees, and over by the far bank when casting left at 45 degrees. The flow varies due to flood control. It fishes best when the current is strongest.

Directions: head for Simancas N620, 10 km southwest of Valladolid. Go over Roman bridge, then take the road for the Peñalba school (*colegio*), follow this road around on to dirt track for 600 metres to the old building with Pesqueruela written on the side. Park under the lone tree for shade. Now walk over sluice gate and carefully descend down right end of concrete terrace to the weir pool swim. Just a few metres around is the beach swim.

Embalse de Encinas, Encinas de Esgueva, fishing reserve (trout *coto*, carp, barbel, pumpkinseed, pike). A day ticket is needed to fish for coarse species. Email Jorge for tickets at kenis@navegalia.com or ask when you buy your licence in Valladolid. Worth the trouble of getting a permit because of the lovely setting. A medium-size reservoir with a good track that navigates the shoreline. It's 15 metres at deepest. Good swims and easy access everywhere. Barbel over 8kg, carp over 15. The use of sweetcorn will spark the interest of the hundreds of lake trout so use boilies, to which the carp respond very well. But the use of a light fly tackle would prove great fun to catch the trout. Accommodation: Casa Paco Restaurante/Hotel Rural, C/Mayor, 30, Encinas de Esgueva. Directions: head northeast VA140 to Encinas de Esgueva. Head out of town, signposted for reservoir, 1,600 metres along dirt track. Worth a stopover because of all the good points mentioned.

Embalse de San José, Río Duero, Castronuño, free fishing (carp, barbel). A top Duero fishery. For tickets to some sections: Bar in Villafranco de Duero, otherwise free. The best place to fish is on north bank up by the railway bridge. Here there are 35 free *pesquils* (platforms) to choose from. The first two nearest the bridge offer disabled access. Luncheon meat is first-choice bait. There are some nice common carp up to 15kg. Barbel also reach a good size. This is a popular spot with visiting anglers from Zamora and Valladolid. They are very friendly and usually offer a slice of melon or a cold beer by way of introduction to the Spanish angling fraternity. Accommodation: Casa Pepe, in town. Camping is not permitted in the park area by the swims but tolerated immediately below the dam. www.castronuno.com or email: tourismo@castronuno.com Tel: 983 866 095.

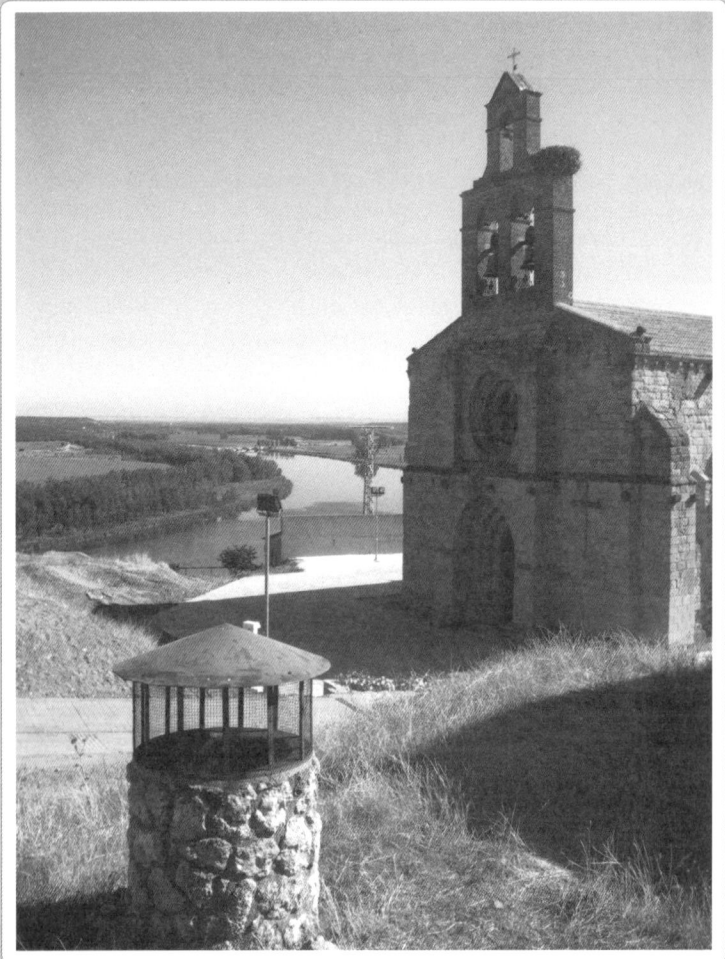

View over Embalse de San José on the Río Duero from Castronuno

Directions: west N122 towards Toro, then south at Villaester for Castronuño. At the dam, cross over to the north side and turn right straight away down a dirt track, sign-posted "Río Duero" for 2km. Follow it past a house and parallel with railway line. Just before railway crossing, take right fork 200 metres onto the *pesquil* area. Park in shady plantation 50 metres from bank.

Río Pisuerga, Valladolid city centre, free fishing (carp, pumpkinseed, crucian pike). Carp over 5kg, average weight is 3kg. This river stretch is much improved vis-à-vis the environment and water quality. Directions: Fish the jetty at La Plaza Tenerias.

Castilla-La Mancha

CHAPTER EIGHT

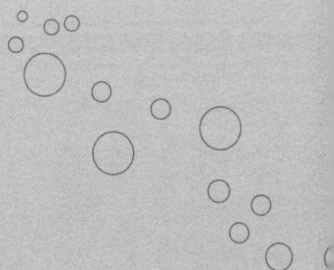

⬇ Castilla-La Mancha

This vast region has bleak, sun-scorched plains but also pleasant mountainous zones and promising wetlands for anglers. The Río Guadiana flows out of the Lagunas de Ruidera and meanders across the region before entering Extremadura. A good general website for the region is www.castillalamancha.es

Licences: Delegación Provincial de la Consejería de Agricultura y Medio Ambiente, C/Tesifonte Gallego, 1, 02071 Albacete. Tel: 967 213 390. Boat licences: Confederación Hidrográfica del Guadiana, C/Sinforiano Medronero, 12, 06011 Badajoz. Tel: 992 421 2100. E-mail: chguadiana@mmma.es. Visit: www.chguadiana.es. Only rowing boats permitted on some lakes.

Angling information: Federación Castellanomanchega de Pesca, C/Duque de Lerma, 5, 45004 Toledo. Tel/fax: 925 256 770. E-mail: fedpescaclm@inicia.es. For more information, contact the local angling expert, Antonio Márquez. E-mail: ossa@marca.es.

Visit www.lagunasruidera.com/index2.shtml for information on accommodation and restaurants.

Guadiana bass fishermen have their own club, Guadiana Bass Masters, in Ciudad Real. Tel: 926 219 014.
Email: guadianabassmaster@wanadoo.es

> Lagunas de Ruidera is a delightful spot - 15 lakes covering 3,772 hectares. The mysterious Montesinos cave described in *Don Quixote* is located nearby

Lagunas de Ruidera, Ruidera, free fishing (carp, *comizo* barbel, black bass, pike, trout, eels, pumpkinseed). This is a delightful beauty spot, an oasis amid the parched plains of La Mancha. A series of 15 lakes covering 3,772 hectares, with an average depth of six metres. The largest is 4km long. Out of these lakes flows the Río Guadiana. The mysterious Montesinos cave described by Cervantes in his classic tale *Don Quixote* is located nearby.

Crystal-clear waters, some turquoise blue, in wonderful surroundings make this area a hit with weekend and summer visitors from Madrid and Albacete. So it's advisable to fish here during the week and avoid peak holiday periods.

Each lake is different with its own head of fish and particular tactics to catch them. All of the following *lagunas* (lakes) permit angling: Tinaja, San Pedro, Redondilla, Lengua, Salvadora, Santos Morcillo, Batana, Colgada, del Rey and Cueva Morenilla. From the high zone down to the Presa de Peñarroya are the Blanca, Conceja, Tomilla, Coladilla and Cenagosa lakes. No fishing from a boat on these.

In the Laguna de la Colgada the carp are especially partial to fish-based boilies. One specimen carp to 15kg was caught near the bar-restaurant using floating crust at dusk. Pike up to 12kg fall to rapid shad Rapalas retrieved at 4 metres depth. The Laguna de San Pedro has carp, crucians, barbel and magnificent fighting black bass. Bloodworm is a killer bait on this lake. The Laguna La Lengua has plenty of black bass. In Conceja, black bass reach 2kg and pike up to 10kg.

One of the best locations to fish is the opening of the last lake, Lago de Cenagosa where it meets the tail-end of the Embalse de Peñarroya, particularly by the rocky inlet. Here, *comizo* barbel have been caught to 16kg. You can catch these big barbel using naturally coloured spoons because the water is so clear. Vinyls also work well.

Why not visit the nearby Embalse de Peñarroya, just to the north of the *lagunas*? Fish in the tail and by the dam, for good-size pike and black bass. There is an abundance of carp here. A little further away, the Embalse de Bolarque has very good access with lots of pike up to 8kg caught on spinning plugs with simple colours.

Directions: halfway between Albacete and Ciudad Real on the N430. From Madrid head south on the A4 (E5), then at Manzanares go east on the N430.

El Tablazo, Reserva de Pesca, Río Júcar, Cuenca (trout to 4kg). Stock lake covering 8,000 square metres. Located next to a hotel. Any type of angling is allowed, including baits and floats. It's a great place to practise fly-fishing because of the varied conditions the lake offers. A river enters via a waterfall at one end of the lake and flows out the other end. Three floating barrages are provided for anglers as well as a central island for casting into the current. There are deep holes and weedy zones. Orange streamers work well here.

This popular angling location is best visited during the week to avoid crowds. October through March there are far less visitors about but the centre is open only at weekends. Catching a large tagged trout that the authorities stock at the lake during low season will secure a prize e.g. one day's free angling. Good luck!

Two-tier system: *Pesca con muerte* – 9 euros per day including first kilo of trout caught, thereafter 4.8 euros for every extra kilo of trout killed. Or *Pesca sin muerte* – 15 euros per day.

Directions: The city of Cuenca is 200km west of Valencia and 160km east of Madrid. From Cuenca head north 20km on CM2105 to Villalba de la Sierra. Address: El Tablazo, Camino de la Noria, s/n, Villalba de la Sierra (Cuenca). Tel/fax: 969 281 488.

Purchase your angling licence at: Delegación Provincial de Medio Ambiente in Cuenca, tel: 969 178 300. Minimum age is 14, minors up to 18 must seek permission from an adult. Over-65s qualify for a free licence.

For more information visit: http:// www.eltablazopescadeportiva.com

Canary
Islands

La Palma
Tenerife   Santa Cruz
Lanzarote
Fuerteventura
Ferro
Isla de la
Gomera
Las
Palmas
Gran Canaria

Balearic Islands

Majorca

Minorca

Palma de Mallorca

Isla de Cabrera

Ibiza

Isla de Formentera

Canary Islands and Balearics

CHAPTER NINE

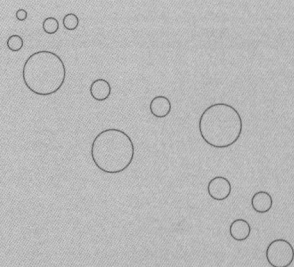

⬇ Gran Canaria

Purchase your freshwater fishing licence at: Consejería de Política Territorial y Medio Ambiente: C/Profesor Agustín Millares Carló, 18, Edificio Usos Múltiples, 35071 Las Palmas. Tel: 928 306 000; or at the Cabildo de Gran Canaria in Las Palmas. Tel: 928 385 003. Fax: 928 367 124.

Embalse de Chira, Gran Canaria (carp). Ron Woodward, an angler with plenty of experience of fishing these islands, describes his favourite spot. Readers can contact Ron for more information on the Chira reservoir at ron@anglinglines.com

"This lake was formed about 30 years ago by damming a ravine in the mountains to trap the rainfall. The reservoir is used for irrigation purposes as well as supplying water to the holiday resorts lower down the island. Carp were initially introduced to control the weed problem.

> "When fishing the Canaries I would advise you to step up the specification of your tackle. Use snag leaders because the bottom is extremely rocky"

Fish to the features around the lake. The depth varies greatly from one metre, dropping off quickly to 10 metres only a couple of rod lengths out, and up to 30 metres at the dam. Look over the other side of the dam wall if you wish to get some idea of how deep the lake is. On the roadside there are many different types of swims. It is possible to drive straight up to the shoreline and more or less fish out of the back of your car. I have had good bags of carp and decent-sized fish from most areas.

Fish float or ledger: Fishing ledger, I prefer to fish close in between two to five metres. I have found that carp will take most floating baits, e.g. bread, dog biscuits, chum mixer etc. off the top in the margins.

Tackle: When fishing in the Canaries, I would advise you to step up the specification of your tackle. Use snag leaders because the bottom is extremely rocky. Take a waterproof covering for your bed chair. This comes in handy when night fishing and it also converts the bed chair into an unhooking mat when required, thus reducing your baggage weight.

PHOTOS ON THIS PAGE COURTESY OF TERRY JORDAN

Embalse de Chira, Gran Canaria

Terry Jordan with a 15lb carp at Lake Chira

Permits: Make sure you obtain the special fishing permit as this allows you to fish with more than one rod and at night. Camping is permitted on private land by the lake with the owners' consent. Alternatively, Agustín Pérez Cabrera can obtain this licence for you in advance and organise local accommodation and provide bait. His address is Cercados de Araña 129, Presa de Chira, San Bartolomé de Tirajana, Gran Canaria. Tel: 620 967 863. Email: chirafish@hotmail.com. He speaks perfect English.

Directions: Embalse de Chira, along with several of the lakes on the island, is in the centre of Gran Canaria. To get to Chira, turn left out of Las Palmas airport on the 812 towards Playa del Inglés. Stay on this road until you have passed through San Augustín and are entering Playa del Inglés. From here, leave the 812 and head towards Fatiga. Follow this road until you reach San Bartolomé, a small town in the centre of the island. Go through the town centre, make for La Plata and look for a turning on the left signposted Embalse de Chira. Follow this to the lake. A word of warning: the drive to the lake can be a bit scary so take care if it is your first time.

I recommend that you eat and drink at the friendly local bars and restaurants, situated only a few minutes' walk from the lake. Entering La Plata, you will see on your right a large supermarket just off the road. This sells bait for the lake, i.e. maize, chickpeas, sweetcorn. Believe me, I have caught more carp in Chira on baits like sweetcorn, than I ever have on boilies."

Embalse de Cueva de las Niñas, San Bartolomé de Tirajana (carp). Located just about in the middle of the island, this 300-hectare reservoir offers very easy fishing for smaller carp that reach 8 to 10 kg. For non-stop action this could be the place to go. Permits for fishing as well as for camping at the water have to be purchased in Las Palmas in advance.

Embalse de Ayagaures (carp). Located in the south of the island. Small number of fish to large size, 15kg and over. Fishing can prove technical. Night fishing permitted. Permits can be obtained in Las Palmas.

↓ Tenerife

Licences and Information: Federación Canaria de Pesca, Puerta Canesca, 49, Edif. Jamaica A2, Planta A, 38003 Santa Cruz de Tenerife. Tel: 922 240 219; Consejería de Política Territorial y Medio Ambiente, Rambla General Franco, 149, Edificio Mónaco, 38078 Santa Cruz de Tenerife. Tel.: 922 476 200

↓ Balearic Islands

Angling licences: Consejería de Medio Ambiente del Gobierno Balear, Avda. Gabriel Alomar y Villalonga, 33, 07006 Palma de Mallorca. Tel: 971 176 800.

Information: Federación Balear de Pesca, Joan Miró, 325, 07015 Calanova, Palma de Mallorca. Fax: 971 702 088. Email: fbpescaic@telefonica.net

PHOTO COURTESY OF AGUSTIN PÉREZ CABRERA

Embalse de Chira, Gran Canaria

Helpful Hints

CHAPTER TEN

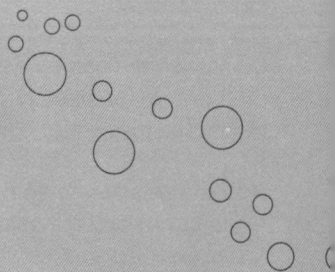

THE ESSENTIAL GUIDE TO COARSE FISHING IN SPAIN

What should I take with me?

A disposable camera to snap your beauties, with a flash for night-time action, Polaroid sunglasses, a visored hat, sun block (temperatures can reach well over 30 degrees C in July and August), mosquito repellent, water containers, a foldable aluminium chair, a brolly to keep the sun off, a torch, binoculars.

Maps: A good map is essential to find your way around. Michelin maps on a scale of 1/400,000 are recommended. Campsa produces an annual guide with maps on a scale of 1:300,000. A map of Catalonia of the same scale is published by the regional government.

Security

Lock your vehicle and put the seats back after unloading. Don't leave your property on display in the car. Always keep your passport, credit cards and money on your person at all times. Take photocopies of important documents and keep in a separate place. Use a money belt. Especially when fishing country swims, be aware of people who are obviously not locals.

River water, though very clear, may not be clean. Ear infections are not unheard-of. Do not go swimming in any of the channels even if you see locals doing so.

On a personal note: in 15 years I have not had any misfortune. At Bitem on the Ebro, for example, the biggest danger comes from the gangster-like mosquitoes – they could steal your hubcaps.

Accommodation in Spain

Good-quality accommodation at reasonable prices is available all over Spain. Even the smallest village usually has something to offer. Ask at the local Oficina de Turismo.

For the cheapest options, keep an eye out for these signs: *Camas*: beds available; *Camas y comidas*: bed and breakfast; *Habitaciones*: rooms to let; *Fonda* (white "F" in square, blue sign): basic pension; *Casa de Huespedes* (a "CH" sign): guest house.

Usually a little more costly are *Pensiones* (a "P" sign) and *Hostales* (an "H" sign, graded one to three stars). In the country you will find many *casas rurales*. These range from budget B&Bs to stylish, pricey establishments.

Hotels range from cheap one-star places to luxury five stars. *Paradores*, state-run hotels, often in historic castles and convents, are worth at least one night's stay. Discounts available for different age groups. Information: www.parador.es and www.tourspain.co.uk. Email: info@parador.es

Spain has many campsites and there shouldn't be a problem finding one near your fishing spot. Camping outside official sites is tolerated, but not in built-up areas and at least 1km away from official sites. Check on possible overnight spots through the Internet. Use Google or Yahoo search engines then enter: Spain accommodation, adding hotels/budget or hostels or your chosen location.

Or visit one of these websites: www.okspain.org (favourite for hotels/campsites all over Spain); www.toprural.com; www.reservations.bookhostels.com; www.turimerural.com (good for self-catering accommodation); www.magictravelgroup.co.uk, www.indiv-travellers.com; www.simply-travel.com (apartments, houses, villas); www.hostel.com (hostels); www.hostelsspain.com (independent hostels); www.ruralandalus.es (rural houses). For camping, try www.infocamping.com/spain/es/html/Cadiz, Almería etc.

At www.angling-in-spain.com Peter Staggs offers angling information and details of fishing holidays at locations all over Spain. For additional information, contact: Spanish Tourist Board, 22/23 Manchester Square, London, W1M 5AP. Tel: 0207 402 8182. Email: londres@tourspain. Or visit www.tourspain.co.uk

Addresses
To understand Spanish addresses, note the following. Street names are written thus C/Pablo Picasso, 25-2a. The "C" stands for *calle* (street), 25 would be the house or block number, "2a" indicates *planta segunda* or second floor. *Bajo* after the house number means ground floor. If the street name is followed by "s/n", it means *sin número* (no number). "Ctra" is short for *carretera* or highway, "Pl." is short for *plaza* (square), and "avda" for *avenida* (avenue). *Apdo*. 166 indicates Post Office Box 166. To call Spain from most European countries, first dial 00 then the country code, 34. Within Spain the first two or three digits indicate which province you are calling. Thus Barcelona numbers always start with 93 and all numbers in Granada province start with 958.

Angling info and the Internet
Excellent information on angling in Spain can be obtained through

the Internet. A useful website for information on the various species is www.fishbase.org. Click on "Spain", then "freshwater species". Even if you can't access the Internet at home, public libraries in the UK provide a free broadband service and cybercafes are to be found everywhere. For Spain in general visit: www.cerespain.com/municipios. html One of the best sites for accessing angling holidays websites can be found at www.fishhoo.com/Guides/Europe/Spain/ Other useful websites for accommodation and travel include: www.travelinginspain. com/; www.travel-library.com/europe/spain;www.parcsdecatalunya. net/debre; and www.castillo.org

To locate individual Spanish locations, use a search engine like Google or Yahoo and enter the place name and the word "angling", e.g. "Alicante angling" or "catfish ebro". Better still, try the Spanish website, www.yahoo.es. For example, enter *"pesca amposta"*. You may not understand all the vocabulary, but the photos of rivers and lakes will be far superior to anything on UK search engine providers. Even the smallest village in Spain is linked by broadband.

There are no hard and fast rules for using search engines. The more you experiment, the better the results. Try different search words and phrases, e.g. *siluro espagne*, *black bass valencia*, *carpa huelva*. On the results page you can click on one of the websites named and this will quickly bring up the information you are looking for.

Scientific references
Conservation Biology Journal, February 2004
Journal of Fish Biology, December, 2002
Fishery Management and Ecology, 2000
www.fishbase.org

Additional help came from Julian Hunter, fish scientist with Inverness Fisheries Department.

Further reading
The Black Bass in America and Overseas by W. H. Robbins, H. R. MacCrimmon.
Lizarralde, The Man Who Fished For Barbel, by John Langridge, Medlar Press.

For all angling questions, contact the author, email:
philippembroke007@hotmail.com

Vocabulary

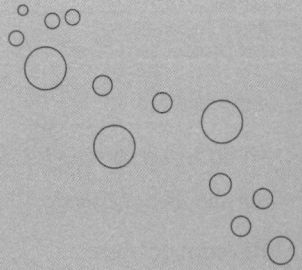

↓ A-Z of Angling in Spain

→ FISH SPECIES

(***** = introduced species)

alburno*: bleak

anguila: eel

blacbás* (or perca americana): largemouth black bass

barbo: barbel

barbo comizo: Iberian barbel

barbo común: snouted Iberian barbel

barbo gitano: gypsy barbel

boga: Iberian nase

bordallo: quart-size carp

brema blanca*: white bream

cacho: chub

cachuelo: pint-sized carp

calandino: chub-like native, Cyprinidae family

cangrejo: American red crab

carpa*: common carp

dorado: goldfish

dorada: gilt-head bream

escardinio/gardí*: rudd

esturión: sturgeon

fiaile: mummichog

gambusino*: mosquitofish

gobio*: gudgeon

jarabugo: Spanish minnow

lisa: thick-lipped grey mullet

lubina: sea bass

lucio*: pike

lucio perca*: zander

madrilla: bleak type

pardilla: mini-carp

perca*: perch

perca sol*, also **pez sol:** pumpkinseed, sun fish

pescadilla: whiting

róbalo: sea bass

rutilo*: roach

sábalo: shad

salmón del Pacífico*: rainbow trout

savelino*: brook trout

siluro*: wels catfish.

tenca: tench

trucha arco iris*: rainbow trout

→ USEFUL WORDS

asticot: maggot

anzuelo: hook

azud: small dam, waterwheel

caña: fishing rod

chufa: tiger nut

confederación hidrográfica: water board

cucharilla: salmon spoon

desembocadura: river mouth, outlet

embalse: reservoir

escala: fish ladder

esclusa: sluice gate

garbanzo: chick pea

gusano: earthworm

huerta: fertile irrigated area

ir de pesca: to go fishing

laguna: lake

masilla: groundbait, with sardines and anchovies

pan duro: hard, stale bread

pantano: artificial lake or marsh

pesca: fishing

pesca sin muerte: sign indicating water where fish must be returned alive

pesca con muerte: water where the killing of fish is allowed

pescado: fish (caught, dead, on sale)

pez: fish (in the water)

pesquil: platform for anglers

pozo: channel hole

puente: bridge

presa: dam (wall)

ribera: river bank, lakeside

señuelo: lure

tortuga: turtle, tortoise, terrapin

tramo: stretch of river

vadear: to wade

vadeador: waders

vara de pescar: fishing rod

vedado: prohibited

→ CATALAN

aiguabarreig: confluence

aigua dolça: fresh water

estany: lake, pond

estanyol: small pool

femelles: barbel

font: spring

llisa, llísera: mullet

naixement: spring, source

pantà: reservoir

pont: bridge

resclosa: weir, lock

riu: river

tram: stretch of water

riera: gully

zona de bany: swimming pool area

⬇ Conversion Chart

When weighing your catches, remember:

1 kilogramme (kg) equals 2.2 pounds (lb)

5 kilogrammes equal 11 pounds

1 pound equals 453 grammes

5 pounds equal 2.25 kilogrammes